"Annie Reiner's exce
expositions of Bion'
ble and deep reflecti
based on first-hand,
acquaintance with Bion himself. Moreover, it is an impressive account of Reiner's own thinking, grounded in many years of clinical work and important theoretical developments. Her thoughts on the natural continuity between Bion's early and late work, the origins of the mind and of thinking, and the presence of the transcendental, spiritual dimension in human experience, are invaluable. Anyone interested in human experience, philosophy and psychoanalysis will surely find in this book much needed, touching and evocative food for thought."

Joshua Durban, *child and adult training and supervising psychoanalyst, Israeli Psychoanalytic Society (IPA), Sackler School of Medicine, psychotherapy program, Tel-Aviv University, Israel*

"There are many books on Bion. This one is different: it captures what is revolutionary about Bion's thinking in a fresh and clear way. Reiner, who was a student of Bion in the 1970s, and is now one of the foremost Bion scholars, traces the origins of his thinking concerning the concept of O from its very beginnings in his work on the selected fact, through his work on the 'no-thing' and 'thoughts without a thinker,' and finally to his most developed conception of O as it informs intuition, which is all that we can know. This is a beautifully written book that captures the imagination of the reader, inviting him or her to think with Reiner about the development of Bion's ideas."

Thomas Ogden, *M.D., San Francisco, member and supervising analyst at the San Francisco Center for Psychoanalysis (SFCP)*

"Dr. Reiner has written a remarkable book, describing essentials of the work of W.R. Bion with unusual clarity. Bion's ideas are explored in depth, and applied to her work with analysands, which is presented in detail, and relevant to the specific theories being discussed."

Michael Paul, *M.D., Los Angeles, member and senior training analyst at the Psychoanalytic Center of California (PCC) and the New Center of Psychoanalysis (NCP)*

W. R. Bion's Theories of Mind

Annie Reiner's introduction to Wilfred Bion's theories of mind presents Bion's intricate ideas in an accessible, original way without compromising their complexity.

Reiner uses comparisons to painting, literature, and philosophy, as well as detailed clinical examples, to provide an experience of Bion's work that can be felt as well as thought. The book explores many of Bion's theoretical and clinical innovations and examines the controversy surrounding his concept of O. Reiner provides evidence of a continuity between Bion's early ideas and his later, more esoteric work.

W. R. Bion's Theories of Mind will be essential reading for psychoanalysts and psychoanalytic candidates, as well as students of psychoanalytic and psychological history, and anyone looking for a readable introduction to Bion's work.

Annie Reiner is a senior faculty member and training analyst at the Psychoanalytic Center of California (PCC) in Los Angeles. Her work was greatly influenced by Wilfred Bion, with whom she studied in the 1970s. She lectures throughout the world, is published in numerous journals and anthologies, and is the author of three psychoanalytic books – *The Quest for Conscience and The Birth of the Mind* (2009), *Bion and Being: Passion and the Creative Mind* (2012), and *Of Things Invisible to Mortal Sight: Celebrating the Work of James S. Grotstein* (editor) (2017). She maintains a psychoanalytic practice in Beverly Hills, California.

Routledge Introductions to Contemporary Psychoanalysis
Aner Govrin, Ph.D.

Series Editor:
Tair Caspi, Ph.D.
Executive Editor

Yael Peri Herzovich
Assistant Editor

"Routledge Introductions to Contemporary Psychoanalysis" is one of the prominent psychoanalytic publishing ventures of our day. It will comprise dozens of books that will serve as concise introductions dedicated to influential concepts, theories, leading figures, and techniques in psychoanalysis covering every important aspect of psychoanalysis.

The length of each book is fixed at 40,000 words.

The series' books are designed to be easily accessible to provide informative answers in various areas of psychoanalytic thought. Each book will provide updated ideas on topics relevant to contemporary psychoanalysis – from the unconscious and dreams, projective identification and eating disorders, through neuropsychoanalysis, colonialism, and spiritual-sensitive psychoanalysis. Books will also be dedicated to prominent figures in the field, such as Melanie Klein, Jaque Lacan, Sandor Ferenczi, Otto Kernberg, and Michael Eigen.

Not serving solely as an introduction for beginners, the purpose of the series is to offer compendiums of information on particular topics within different psychoanalytic schools. We ask authors to review a topic but also address the readers with their own personal views and contribution to the specific chosen field. Books will make intricate ideas comprehensible without compromising their complexity.

We aim to make contemporary psychoanalysis more accessible to both clinicians and the general educated public.

For more information about this series, please visit:www.routledge.com/Routledge-Introductions-to-Contemporary-Psychoanalysis/book-series/ICP

W. R. Bion's Theories of Mind

A Contemporary Introduction

Annie Reiner

Routledge
Taylor & Francis Group

LONDON AND NEW YORK

Cover image: © Michal Heiman, *Asylum 1855–2020, The Sleeper* (video, psychoanalytic sofa and Plate 34), exhibition view, Herzliya Museum of Contemporary Art, 2017

First published 2023
by Routledge
4 Park Square, Milton Park, Abingdon, Oxon OX14 4RN

and by Routledge
605 Third Avenue, New York, NY 10158

Routledge is an imprint of the Taylor & Francis Group, an informa business

British Library Cataloguing-in-Publication Data
A catalogue record for this book is available from the British Library

Library of Congress Cataloging-in-Publication Data
Names: Reiner, Annie, author.
Title: W.R. Bion's theories of mind : a contemporary introduction / Annie Reiner.
Description: Abingdon, Oxon ; New York, NY : Routledge, 2023. | Series: Routledge introductions to contemporary psychoanalysis | Includes bibliographical references and index.
Identifiers: LCCN 2022022296 | Subjects: LCSH: Bion, Wilfred R. (Wilfred Ruprecht), 1897–1979. | Psychoanalysis. | Psychoanalytic interpretation.
Classification: LCC BF173 .R436 2023 | DDC 150.19/5—c23/eng/20220729
LC record available at https://lccn.loc.gov/2022022296

ISBN: 978-0-367-74566-0 (hbk)
ISBN: 978-0-367-74568-4 (pbk)
ISBN: 978-1-003-15850-9 (ebk)

DOI: 10.4324/9781003158509

Typeset in Times New Roman
by Apex CoVantage, LLC

Contents

Foreword

In being asked by editors Aner Govrin and Tair Caspi to write about Bion in this series of books by Routledge about prominent figures in psychoanalysis, I did not want only to repeat what Bion had already said, far better than I can, nor did I want to repeat what others had said *about* what Bion had said. It seems more fruitful to focus on some of the mysteries to which he drew our attention, including the transcendent, enigmatic, infinite reality he called "O." The confusion and controversy surrounding this concept may have distracted us from the fact that the real mystery was not only O, but the enigmatic, unknowable, infinite aspects of the human mind able to have an experience of the numinous O. Bion wrote: "The development of the mind has been a frightful nuisance and has caused an awful lot of trouble. I think we are still frightened of it" (1978a, p. 53).

The mind has always been the subject of psychoanalytic inquiry, and here I examine some of the ways Bion deepened the meaning of it, even redefining what we mean by "mind."

Bion expressed concern that the great authority of Freud or Klein, and I think also himself, would become a "barrier to studying people . . . a barrier against revolution" (1979, p. 331). Implicit in this is the idea of psychoanalysis as an unsettling process of learning, as it continues to challenge and change our thinking about this ultimately unknowable mind, thereby upsetting our illusions of safety in what we already know. He called attention to how our familiar but often ossified theories may remove the sense of danger, but also the vitality, from our explorations of the mind.

James Grotstein once kindly described me as "high among Bion scholars," high praise indeed from such a world-renowned Bion scholar as he, but I hope what I describe here is more about being a scholar of the states of mind that Bion addressed, including the capacity for the deeply intuitive state of mind of O that allows us temporarily to transcend what we already know and make contact with new ideas that help us, and our patients, continue learning and growing.

Bion's Early and Late Periods

I also explore the ideas that comprise what are sometimes called Bion's early and late periods. While they are usually believed to be so different as to have little relationship to each other, I describe what I agree are significantly different states of mind depicted in his early and later work but that are nonetheless importantly and intimately related, though not necessarily in obvious ways.

Bion's "early period" roughly spans his writings from the 1940s through the early 1960s, including his work on groups and his theories of thinking. The "late period" from the mid-1960s through the 1970s includes numerous books of published lectures from South America, London, France, New York, and Los Angeles and the maturation of many earlier ideas in *Attention and Interpretation*, most notably the concept of O, as well as Bion's (1991) fictionalised autobiographical trilogy, *Memoir of the Future*, written in the mid- to late 1970s. The most polarising of his ideas is his concept of O, the central idea of his late work, which Bion considered to be the essential psychoanalytic perspective for doing clinical work. While many admirers of his early theories of thinking were not admirers of the later work, I explore what I see as an essential continuity between these two periods. The following anecdote includes a statement Bion made to me in a private meeting in Los Angeles in 1977 that provides evidence for this idea.

I was a very young psychotherapist at the time and contacted Bion hoping he would agree to teach a private clinical seminar for me and four of my colleagues, all young psychotherapists and psychoanalytic candidates. I arranged to meet with him in his office in Beverly Hills to discuss this. For someone so young, and so painfully aware of how little I knew, I was surprised by how unusually free and comfortable I felt in his presence, which I attributed to his rare openness and authenticity. I seemed to feel emboldened to speak up more than was normal for me at the time because I sensed that someone was really listening. At some point in our discussion, I noticed on the shelf a copy of his book *Attention and Interpretation*, and I commented how much the book had meant to me, having already read it numerous times. He paused, then replied, "I think I'm saying the same thing in every book" (Bion, 1977a). Since Bion was not one to speak idly, I took him at his word and eventually began to see that the ideas in that book, written in 1970, were related in some essential ways to much of his earlier writings. There was a line of development, whereby the seeds of the later work, while not yet fully developed, were often present, and with each book they grew into what he became more fully able to perceive and express over time.

Bion's focus was always on the unknowable mystery of the mind toward which his curiosity led him. His concept of O finally provided a more direct way to communicate about it. And so, while O is the most revolutionary and controversial of his later ideas, it is not an anomaly in his overall opus but rather a kind of hub that eventually connected many of his other ideas. In Chapters 5 and 6, I address the relationship between O and earlier theories like beta and alpha elements, the "no-thing," the "selected fact," etc. While the relationship may not be causal or direct, it is nonetheless significant. Some of the earlier theories help us see O in a slightly different light, and O reveals a new perspective on the importance of those earlier ideas to psychoanalytic work. While all roads do not lead directly to O, many of those theories are precursors to deeply intuitive states of mind that Bion ultimately called O. His early idea of maternal "reverie" is one simple example of precursor to O in that it reflects the importance of the mother's capacity for a state of at-one-ment with her infant, the mother's mind as a sort of metaphysical extension of the infant's mind.

Bion (1962a) writes, "Reverie is a factor of the mother's alpha-function" (p. 36), and so we might say that in this state of at-one-ment, both reverie and alpha function are factors of O that are necessary precursors. Reverie, Grotstein (2007) writes, "strictly designates the purposefully directed and induced state of mind of the analyst who abandons 'memory and desire,'" (p. 185). And as I also examine in Chapters 5 and 6, it is that abandonment of memory and desire that Bion clearly prescribes to facilitate receptivity to the waking dream state of O.

While the need for access to O reflects a quantum leap mentally and clinically, the comment Bion made to me about the similarity between the ideas in all his various books lent credence to the connection between his early and later work. Bion's comment also reminded me of Ezra Pound's statement that every writer has his own small window into truth (Cookson, 1975). Although each writer is driven to express his or her own unique perspective on the world, that fundamental, often unconscious perspective may evolve or deepen over time, thus becoming a different version of that same truth. This was certainly the case with Bion, whose idiosyncratic views often illuminated the ways in which disparate mental energies unite to create order and meaning in the healthy mind. Early on, Bion (1962a) speaks of "binocular vision," two eyes needed to correlate a view of a single object, which he compared to the mental need for correlation "of conscious and unconscious in viewing a psycho-analytic object" (p. 86). I examine other of his theories about the relationships of opposites as well, like container and contained, and the oscillations of Ps ↔ D, relationships between opposing experiences that are also necessary to thinking and to healthy mental functioning.

There is also what Bion ended up describing as the necessary relationship between the ephemeral, infinite, unknowable realm of absolute truth or ultimate reality – O – and the finite realm of knowledge – K. Even the transcendent, unthinkable experiences of O must be paired with an antithetical partner, K, in order to transform those transcendent intuitions into interpretations that can be verbally communicated to the patient. Bion's early works laid a necessary foundation for a kind of mind able to contain something of that ultimately uncontainable, indescribable realm. This mind is not an intellectual phenomenon but rather is based on a numinous experience of a dream-like state of mind that we embody but cannot ourselves understand.

Introduction

Revolutionary Change

Bion's work inspired a psychoanalytic revolution, the parameters of which are probably still unknown and the challenges of which are still unmet. Although the influences of Freud and Melanie Klein, his second analyst, formed the basis of his psychoanalytic foundation, his unflagging curiosity and unique vision soon led him to build upon that foundation with new perspectives on mental life and the development of the capacity to think that are examined in this book.

> Let us hope that such a thing as a mind, a personality, a character exists, and that we are not just talking about nothing.
>
> (Bion, 1976, p. 317)

Here, Bion fearlessly questions the most basic aspect of psychoanalytic inquiry, the existence of the mind itself, shining a light on the mysterious darkness in which psychoanalytic work takes place by virtue of its metaphysical nature. But this also represents a challenge in our relationship to language itself, for while we blithely use words like "mind," assuming we agree on its meaning, upon closer inspection we find that since these words reflect a metaphysical realm, unmanifest in the physical world of the senses, we may not actually know what each of us means by it. Bion regularly takes us face to face with our own ignorance.

DOI: 10.4324/9781003158509-1

Catastrophic Change

Bion's concept of "catastrophic change" foreshadowed the difficulties his own challenging ideas would pose for the psychoanalytic community. It was evident in the reactions I saw in his audiences in Los Angeles, who were often disturbed by Bion's tendency to respond to questions in ways that seemed to them oblique or withholding. His tendency to leave space for people to think for themselves seemed evasive to some, or purposefully confusing, and others wondered if he was psychotic. What I saw was someone who was exquisitely observant, in the way that children are observant, questioning everything, even what we as grown-ups may think is obvious. This encouraged a capacity to see the mystery in things, to see with a child's eye that the answers are not really so obvious to us after all.

Although I most certainly did not understand all I heard at Bion's lectures early on, what I did hear in them was the ring of truth. I sensed the depth of what he was saying, much as an infant "understands" the music of language before knowing its lexical meaning.

This book is not an attempt to provide a comprehensive survey of Bion's theories but instead explores the essence of some of his most important theories, highlighting their relationships to each other and to his opus as a whole. Nor are Bion's theories necessarily presented chronologically. For instance, Chapter 1 is devoted to Bion's ideas about language, which figured prominently in his later work, but since verbal language is so fundamental to psychoanalytic work, it seemed like a good place to start. Ideas from Bion's "early period" –including "alpha function," "beta elements," the "no-thing," and the "selected fact," as well as later ideas of "thoughts without a thinker" – are examined in Chapters 1, 2, 3, and 4. The revolutionary aspect of Bion's (1970) work is most evident in the controversy surrounding his later concept of O, representing absolute truth, ultimate reality, the infinite, and the godhead. O, the centrepiece of his later work, is discussed in depth in Chapters 5 and 6. It warrants this attention in part because of its role, according to Bion (1970), as the fundamental perspective without which psychoanalysis cannot be practiced. Bion's relatively early idea of the "selected fact" describes a harmonising principle that helps give coherence to otherwise incoherent, often chaotic elements in a session. Given my proposal that this higher elusive unknowable truth – O – is essentially, and unintentionally, the hub that connects his theories as a whole, we might say that O is the "selected fact" of Bion's work that helps organise and give new meaning to the rest.

Many of Bion's ideas deepen our understanding of previous theories, whether his own or other analysts'. They offer a sort of tune-up, revealing questions we have about theories that may have become familiar and stale and prevent us from discovering what we still need to learn. Expressing his concern about our ability to remain open in this way and our need to vitalise our theoretical understanding, Bion wrote: "Will psycho-analysts study the living mind? Or is the authority of Freud to be used as a deterrent, a barrier to studying people? The revolutionary becomes respectable – a barrier against revolution" (Bion, 1979, p. 331).

A new idea is always a revolution in the mind. Even adding to or amending already existing laws can be a form of destroying them, for as we step away from what we know, everything is cast in a new light. Old ossified truths, enshrined as dogma, become barriers against whatever dangerous new truths we have yet to learn. Each session is a new reality. None of the psychoanalytic texts we read are about this particular patient's interaction with this particular analyst, the particular reality, O, to which Bion suggested we remain open. "Resistance," Bion wrote, "is resistance to O." This focus on what is new is of primary significance in psychoanalysis, which is built upon the need for mental change.

Likewise, we cannot simply learn and repeat what others have to say *about* Bion, including what I say here, but rather must stay focused on the always unknown aspect of the mind that was the subject of his inquiry. Bion was typically realistic about this unsettling task.

Some people may be frightened of Bion's ideas without recognising that what is actually feared is the uncertainty of a vast, unknowable human mind beyond our control.

Chapter 1

Limitations of Language in the Psychic Realm

Bion had a reputation for being enigmatic, mysterious, complex, and confusing. While I found him at times to be all of those things, at the same time his vision often derived from the simplest of perceptions, including how we speak and use language.

Following a case presentation in a clinical seminar I attended, Bion (1977b) asked, "What language is this patient speaking?" This enigmatic question sounded like a Zen koan that cannot be answered logically, but since language and verbal communication are fundamental tools in psychoanalysis, the question was an important one, and it forced the group to open our minds to a different, intuitive realm of thinking. Bion was calling attention to the vagaries of a language created for the *physical* world of the senses but which analysts must apply to the *metaphysical* world of the mind. For instance, the simplest sentence, like referring to Bion's "vision" or "view," uses a sense-based metaphor when in fact we do not *view* thoughts at all. Neither thoughts nor feelings have physical attributes, they cannot be seen, touched, smelled, etc., and yet we must find a way to talk to people about these ephemeral mental states. We use metaphors like "Something about this person smells fishy" to express a feeling we have of something suspicious or distasteful, and we are so familiar with these metaphors that we don't think twice about them. It becomes more difficult, however, when dealing with increasingly deep emotional states.

Upon being asked whether the analyst ever does anything except talk, Bion (1977c) replied, "Yes, he remains silent" (p. 29). Silence has an important role in analysis, for one has to take time to feel,

DOI: 10.4324/9781003158509-2

and think, and keep observing without preconceived ideas, in order to detect the underlying meaning of a session. The use of language presented a challenge as complex as the mind it sought to talk about, and Bion's focus on language essentially questioned the efficacy of the tools of our trade, which he suggested may not be up to the job. Regarding our communications with psychoanalytic colleagues, Bion wrote:

> We often talk in a way which sounds exactly as if we talked the same language. It is very doubtful.
>
> (Bion, 1975, p. 23)

Language, he was suggesting, is more complex than we think, and clearly, for him, it was time to think about it. When it came to the obstacles in communicating with patients, Bion (1977b) asked, "How can we get the interpretation to the right address?" This implied uncertainty as to whether or not the analyst was actually being heard by the patient. Many psychoanalysts, including Ferenczi (1932), Klein (1921), Bion (1963a), Winnicott (1960), and others, began dealing with increasingly primitive mental states, and Bion's discussions about language reflect the recognition of need for a language that could speak to those deeper levels of the mind, before or beyond words. The impediments to being understood are not always evident to the analyst or the analysand, but they are serious, and so I decided to devote this first chapter to Bion's ideas about the central role of language in psychoanalysis.

Everyone Can Talk

Verbal language is a distinctly human capacity, and since almost everyone can talk, we assume that we can do so effectively. As Bion pointed out, the language of psychoanalysis and emotional life differs from the language of everyday language, and yet we use the same fundamental language for both. Our assumptions that we will be understood may not be warranted, for as Bion (1992) wrote, "The language of ordinary human beings is only appropriate to the rational" (p. 371). Grotstein (2007) similarly writes, "Bion seems to be saying that ordinary (sense-based) language is unsuitable for use in psychoanalysis"

(p. 111). Discussions about language figured prominently in Bion's later ideas about metaphysical realities of the mind, and because neither the mind nor its contents (feelings, thoughts, ideas) has physical attributes, he went so far as to question how we know that the mind exists at all.

> Let us hope that such a thing as a mind, a personality, a character exists, and that we are not just talking about nothing.
>
> (Bion, 1976, p. 317)

Bion never shied away from fundamental questions, and this statement gives voice to the mystery at the heart of psychoanalytic inquiry, namely whether the "mind" (a term he used synonymously with self, character, and personality) even exists. Although Bion himself believed in the existence of this enigmatic mind, he was unconvinced that it was something that analysts had agreed upon, in part because the existence of such an ineffable, metaphysical entity is unprovable through sensory means. While some think that dealing with this enigmatic realm makes psychoanalysis unscientific, for Bion it meant that a new science of the mind was necessary, one that could encompass psychoanalytic knowledge. O was his attempt to do so, but this would require of the analyst "a peculiar state of mind . . . [where] the margin between being consciously awake . . . and being asleep, is extremely small" (Bion, 1978b, p. 41). What kind of mind is that, and what language does it speak?

Clinical Considerations

How is one to detect, in the analyst or analysand, the presence or absence of a sentient mind? The analyst may need to be in a state that is half awake and half asleep, but the patient may be totally asleep and so unable really to understand the interpretations. Patients may show up, and appear to hear and even agree with our interpretations, but we might notice that they seem unmoved or that nothing changes. While this may reflect resistance, envy, or negative therapeutic reactions to change, it may mean that the patient has not yet developed a mind or self that can be present or digest what we say. Winnicott (1974) describes the patient's "fear of breakdown" as a breakdown in infancy that cannot be remembered. He says, "This thing of the past has not happened yet because the patient was not there for it to happen to" (p. 105). The self or mind, that is, was then unborn and remains unborn. Apropos of language, Ferenczi (1988) much earlier addressed a similar matter, "We talk about splitting of the personality but do not seem sufficiently to appreciate the depths of these splits" (p. 199). The words, then, don't accurately express the obstacle of how to speak to the split or splintered parts of a self, a predicament also expressed in Bion's (1977b) question about "how to get the interpretation to the right address." The analyst will need a language able to communicate with that split or unborn self – to become a midwife, as it were, for a psychical birth.

Transcendent Truths and Unconscious Lies

This clinical challenge is born of the need to find a language that can traverse the obstacle of an undeveloped self. The analyst first has to distinguish truth from lies, which sounds simple enough, but these are mental lies that the individual him- or herself may not know are lies. People may be dominated by these unconscious "lies," the illusions, delusions, and other defences that make it difficult or impossible to use their minds in the service of truths their minds cannot contain. These unconscious "lies" are familiar to us in Winnicott's distinction between the True and False Self, whereby problems in the emotional environment – like the mother's depression, neglect, etc. – can obstruct the development of the infant's True, authentic self, which is then replaced by a False Self. "The infant lives, but lives falsely" (Winnicott, 1960, p. 146). This can result in the individual's entire self becoming a lie, for "only the True Self can be creative and only the True Self can feel real" (ibid., p. 148).

The word "lie" may seem misleading if one attaches to it a conscious intention or a moral judgement, but these are unintentional, unconscious "untruths," originally meant as protection from pain, but they distort one's perceptions, and one's fundamental identity as the True Self is hidden even from the infant himself. It is a kind of mental death, and if this False Self dominates, the analyst may be talking to a *physically* present patient who does not *psychically* exist. Again, how can one speak to, or be heard by, a non-existent self? The putative language of that absent or unborn self is significantly different from the language of an authentic self. The overt language of the False Self is, of course, still English or French, Spanish, Portuguese, etc., but it is only superficially the same language – same words, different language, for the aim of one is to communicate, while the unconscious aim of the other is to obstruct communication. Like Bion's question, "What language is this patient speaking?" – can one speak authentically if one's language cannot communicate the truth or meaning of a self that does not exist?

Clinical Vignette

One brief example of the mind or self as yet unborn is a patient who recently complained of not being able to sleep, waking up multiple times a night and unable to get back to sleep. He mentioned some things that were causing anxiety and lamented, "I used to be such a good sleeper." He spoke about other things, a fight with his girlfriend, rage at his boss (and rage was a central issue for him), but one sentence continued reverberating in my ears – "I used to be such a good sleeper." I said, "You used to be such a good sleeper, and then you came here and something woke up." What had awakened in the last four years of analysis were his feelings of sadness, abandonment, and vulnerability that used to be instantly killed off with rage. Not yet knowing quite what to do with these new feelings, he is nostalgic for the good old days when he was sound asleep.

Language of Achievement and Language of Substitution

These ideas are reflected in Bion's (1970) distinction between the "Language of Achievement" and the "Language of Substitution." The former is a means of expressing psychical states, as one needs to do in psychoanalysis, while the latter is valid only for sensory-based language that Bion described as a "debased currency, words which are worn absolutely smooth till they are meaningless". He includes in the Language of Substitution the often overly theoretical language of psychoanalysis and instead advises the need for each analyst "to [forge] his own language" (Bion, 1976, p. 315).

Language of Achievement and Language of Substitution

Bion's Language of Achievement was inspired by Keats's idea of "Negative Capability."

> It struck me what quality went to form a "Man of Achievement," especially in Literature & which Shakespeare possessed so enormously – I mean *Negative Capability*, that is, when a man is capable of being in uncertainties, mysteries, doubts, without any irritable reaching after fact or reason.
>
> (Keats, 1817, p. 329, italics in original)

"Negative Capability" – relinquishing control and one's need for answers in order to exist in the uncertain mystery and open-minded intuition Keats describes – is the basis of Bion's Language of Achievement, but it is also essential to Bion's concept of O. Artists, writers, and poets often describe this state of mind as a sense that their work is being created by an Other – the Muse, or God – but on a human level it is represented by the secular version of the awesome mystical state of O that Bion called the "godhead." We more closely examine Bion's association with that intuitive mystical state in the chapters on O, but a similar idea is expressed here by Plato:

> The deity has bereft [poets] of their senses and uses them as ministers. . . . Poets are nothing but interpreters of the gods.
>
> (Plato, 1961, p. 220)

Briefly put, poets relinquish their minds to better express that divine mind, much like divesting the mind of memory, desire, and understanding in order to be in touch with O and the capacity to live, like of the Man of Achievement, "in mysteries, doubts and uncertainty."

Bion (1970) described the Language of Achievement as "both prelude to action and itself a kind of action" (p. 125). These are not mental actions like projections that evacuate feelings and mental states but the vital energy of a mind able to tolerate the helplessness of not knowing, which paradoxically facilitates the potency of a mind able to think. Like Milton's (1652) idea, "He also serves who stands and waits"

(p. 107), this apparent passivity is a humble submission to Fate, the same unmanifest "Negative Capability" in the Language of Achievement and in the language of poets who cede their senses to the "gods."

How does one address an absent self when the false self knows nothing of the true self or its needs? The false self gets proficient at faking a common language, but it lacks resonance. People copy observed behaviour – monkey see, monkey do – but its lack of meaning makes the analysis feel meaningless as well.

In this clinical vignette, the first "address" I had to find for the patient was her *non*-address, so she could begin to be aware of her unconscious absence and we could begin creating a language based on these deeper truths.

Clinical Vignette

"Mrs. C," a bright, successful businesswoman, was deeply scarred by abandonment from her needy, depressed mother. About two years into her analysis, Mrs. C described dreams in which, "I keep trying to find solutions to problems that don't exist." It seemed like a good description of the activities, and the language, of an absent self.

> *I dreamt I was at work, re-calculating budgets, endless calculations. I worked hard all night long. When I woke up I thought, "These aren't real problems . . . none of this is real."*

I told Mrs. C that despite her tireless calculations, she cannot tell what anything is worth, including herself. As a child, her mother's mindlessness made her feel alternately worthless and enraged, but without a mind to contain and make meaning of these feelings, they went round and round within her mind, and still do, for despite her hard work and determination, she has no way of knowing what is happening inside her. We have come to refer to this as "being on the hamster wheel," with thoughts that go nowhere, as she goes endlessly back and forth between feeling worthless and enraged at her mother's worthlessness and then back again to her own guilt and worthlessness for hating her mother.

This endless loop about her own worth was transformed in her dream into something quantifiable – money – but Mrs. C's endless budgetary computations cannot solve the emotional question of her value to her mother and, ultimately, her right to exist. As this began to be real to her, she became anxious about dying, which often accompanies a mental birth, for as her feelings awakened, so did her awareness of her dead self. It was a good sign, because one cannot fear death if one is already mentally dead or absent. The first "address" I had to find for Mrs. C was her *non*-address, the place where she did not exist, where her feelings were dead. As this absence became painfully real, we began creating a language that had meaning to us both.

Mrs. C was speaking a language in which concrete, quantifiable money substitutes for the ephemera of emotional reality. She was engaged in meaningless debates with herself that lack the power to help her experience or think about her feelings. This non-language for a non-existent problem, created by a mind as yet unable to feel or think or exist, is a language that mimics logic but lacks meaning. As she began feeling her feelings, she could feel the emptiness and lack of meaning, and, while painful, it was an experience of truth and inherent meaning.

Clinical Example – "Roberta" (Session 1)

"Roberta" began analysis ten years ago, complaining of anxiety, obsessive sexual thoughts, and promiscuous behaviour. She had a successful business, having systematically set and fulfilled professional and personal goals that fuelled a sense of superiority over others. She lacked emotional involvement with people, and I often felt a sense of emptiness in her presence. As tender feelings began to arise in analysis, she felt ashamed and paranoid, convinced that I revelled in having power over her. This changed slowly, over many years, but real feelings of vulnerability, need, or gratitude are still often followed by days or weeks of hostility and distrust. Her relationships with men were highly sexualised, but she recently met a man she respected and loved, although intermittently, as she had the same problems there sustaining connection.

Her painful awareness of her deadness and absence of a real self was evident in a recent *dream about a colleague with nothing of her own self, who borrowed everything from other people.* Her ability to dream this indicated her growing awareness of her frightening sense of nothingness. When I interpreted this, she changed the subject, then said, "I don't like hearing it, and I reserve the right to ignore you." This was a direct message from that dead or false self that had always ignored anything real. Apparently, today's interpretation had reached the right address – in a sense, the *absence* of an address – but it was roundly rejected, as was I, and in this session, Roberta began grappling more directly with her growing capacity to need me versus her wish to stay emotionally dead. She had always chosen the latter, for her promiscuity was fun for her, but that sexual excitement has begun to frighten her, as it now ushered in feelings of emptiness, and she was no longer sure which she preferred.

Roberta's Session – Six Months Later

Roberta said she felt good yesterday, in touch with loving feelings for her boyfriend, but this change disturbed her. She awoke today feeling sad, her body almost paralyzed.

> *I dreamt I was with my old high school friends, close friends. We were each going our own way, to different colleges in different parts of the world, although we were our current age. It was sad, going away all by myself . . . maybe to Princeton . . . with just a little bag I carried on my back. I heard an old Black guy saying, "People start out all over again . . . all alone."*

Roberta spoke about her promiscuous ways and getting drunk with these friends in high school. "I rarely see them anymore," she added, "but we had a wonderful Zoom call recently . . . like old times." The old Black man "was like the wise narrator in a show I watched as a child," she said, before mentioning cartoons with hobos carrying their belongings on their backs in a scarf tied to a stick. "Princeton is a great school," she said, "but I have no intention of going back to school."

I thought this dream was about Roberta's sadness at having to leave all her old friends, except in this case these "old friends" represented her promiscuity and drinking that obliterated her and her real feelings. I interpreted that even though those old sexual phantasies had begun to make her feel scared and out of control, she is sad to part with these "old friends" that seemed to protect her throughout her life, especially since she is not yet convinced that feelings of love and connection are her "friends." These are profound changes, and so while Roberta seems to view me in this dream as "Princeton . . . a good school," a place of higher learning, she also points out that she has "no intention of going back to school." This helped me understand why Roberta felt paralysed upon awakening this morning, unable to move, for she is not sure which direction to go in. The old path is no longer attractive, but the new path is unknown, with feelings she fears she won't be able to control with the fragmenting sexualisation.

Discussion of the Case

At these deep levels of confusion between mental existence and non-existence, truth and lies are so entangled that one does not know whom to trust. Even more disturbing is the discovery that it is oneself who cannot be trusted. The cartoons and other associations indicated Roberta's childhood experiences of painful detachment and fragmentation (wandering about like a cartoon hobo), for which her sexual defences later provided temporary solace. In this dream, Roberta faces her dilemma directly. The battle lines are drawn between her "good" old friends, whom she now sees are not good for her, and any *new* friends, including me and her *real* self, that are still unknown. Roberta was reassured by these changes but then expressed concern that she might not be strong enough to realise its promise. I told her that since I don't know the future, I could not say what would happen. I added, however, that what we do know is that we have gotten this far and we are both still willing to work at it. Despite not yet knowing what her life will look like without relying on emotional deadness, there was one thing new in the picture – hope – for at least we were both speaking the same language.

Summary and Conclusions

Bion's focus on language suggests the need to hear, in each session, the subtle distinctions in how patients communicate, for the patient's words can be emotional expressions of states of mental life or death. Bion (1975) wrote, "In psychoanalysis we have to manufacture our means of communication while we are communicating" (p. 39). The language of psychoanalysis is born of the moment, in the relationship with each particular patient, and these improvised communications have no shelf life, they cannot be recycled. Nor can they be effectively recreated, and so our attempts to communicate *about* them are impressionistic at best. "You had to be there," as the saying goes, for what actually happens in a session is unknown except to the two parties that are present, and even for them it is the elusive stuff of dreams. However, if we can communicate in an authentic way, something real and powerful transpires, and although we may not be able fully to capture it, those who live it can share its benefits and its magic.

Chapter 2

The No-Thing

In this chapter, we examine Bion's (1962a, 1970) theory of the "no-thing," which essentially describes the genesis of a thought and the capacity to think. For Bion, the scope of analytic work has to expand to include ways to speak to primitive, proto-mental, or compromised mental states. His ideas about thinking compel us to consider whether or not our interpretations can be received by a patient whose mind may or may not have developed sufficiently to contain emotional reality. These ideas about the requirements of mental development also extend the psychoanalytic perspective beyond the study of mental pathology to include that which constitutes mental health. This is significant clinically, for having a clear idea of what constitutes a healthy mind is crucial in helping patients develop toward it.

Bion's profound curiosity led him to question our prevailing assumptions, including the assumption that the patient comes to analysis with an already developed mind. From his perspective, the human mind is a potential that develops in the presence of certain emotional conditions in the infant's relationship with the mother. Lacking these conditions, mental development, including the capacity to think, is obstructed. Meltzer (1984) writes, "Bion's description of the mind's development attributes to the mother/baby relationship a complexity that is partially absent from Klein's work and totally absent from the Freud/Abraham conception" (p. 68).

Meltzer goes on to say that unlike Freud and Klein, who saw mental development as biologically determined, Bion saw the development of the mind as an "epistemological theory . . . that extrapolates toward wisdom, from ignorance to wisdom" (ibid.). Klein's concept of mental

DOI: 10.4324/9781003158509-3

development was instead seen as structural, "evolving from disintegration to integration . . . [while] Freud's concept . . . is primarily a psycho-sexual one that sees migration of erogenous zones from the mouth to the genitals" (ibid.). The revolutionary nature of Bion's ideas about thinking is evident even in his early work, in this belief that the capacity to think is a work in progress, awaiting further mental evolution.

> "Thinking" . . . is embryonic even in the adult and has yet to be developed fully by the race.
>
> (Bion, 1962a, p. 85)

This brings a new perspective, and new challenges, to the work of psychoanalysis. As seen in this chapter, some of Bion's ideas about the development of thinking, and the idea that the foundation of thinking reflect the notion that the foundation lies in the capacity to process emotions.

The Development of Thinking

For Bion (1962a, 1963a), dreaming is crucial to the development of thinking. The infant's ability to dream transforms its raw experiences into thoughts, a capacity that depends first of all upon the mother's capacity for "reverie," by which she receives and affirms the infant's emotional experiences, an intuitive capacity that provides a model of this dreaming function in the child's mind. While Freud saw the work of dreaming as a means of disguising *unconscious* truths about unwanted, unconscious impulses, Bion (1992) saw dreams as part of the process of thinking, by which *conscious* experiences are made available through dreams to be processed unconsciously. For Bion, this unconscious thinking *is* thinking.

> Freud says Aristotle states that a dream is the way the mind works in sleep: I say it is the way it works when awake.
>
> (Bion, 1959, p. 43)

Bion sees thinking as a function of dreaming and so views dreams as constantly present in the mind even during waking life, a means of processing reality. Grotstein (2007) writes, "Thinking itself is, according to Bion, essentially unconscious" (p. 47).

Beta Elements, Alpha Elements, Alpha Function

Thinking is commonly considered a fundamentally rational activity, but for Bion (1962a, 1963a), thinking originates in the infant's ability to contain raw primitive experiences – "beta elements" – through intuitive dream-like activity he called "alpha function." This transforms those primitive beta elements into "alpha elements" – the building blocks of thinking by which dream images, sounds, narratives, etc. can be used to store memories and create dream thoughts and conscious thoughts (Bion, 1992, p. 181).

Since the basis of thinking resides in a capacity to contain primitive emotional life, disorders of thought also reflect disorders in the ability to feel, or process feelings. All infants clearly have feelings, but only when contained and processed through alpha function is the energy of feelings useful in thinking and storing memories. According to Bion, the relationship between container and contained ($\female\male$) is the basis of capacities to feel and think.

Meltzer says, "Not only does [Bion] place the emotional experience prior to thoughts, he also places thoughts prior to thinking" (Meltzer, 1984, p. 67). Although we generally view thoughts as *products* of a thinking mind, Bion (1962b) writes, "Thinking is a function forced upon the psyche by the pressure of thoughts, and not the other way around" (p. 111). To say that thoughts exist before our ability to think them means that truth exists whether or not we can think it, and because human beings have an instinct for truth, we need to develop a way to process these internal or external realities that confront us. From this point of view, we may have to emend Descartes's (1637) "Cogito ergo sum" to "Sum, ergo cogito," for it is not thinking that creates the self (or sense of existence) but the existence of an emotional self that facilitates the capacity to think.

"No-Thing": Foundation of Thinking or Oblivion

The mother's absence engenders intolerable anxiety in an infant not yet able to tolerate separateness from her life-giving care. That terrifying absence is experienced as a "no-mother" or "no-breast" (Bion, 1962a, 1970). Unable to process this mentally, the child may resort to hallucination, sucking one's thumb, for instance, to recreate the absent breast, now felt to be present and within one's control. If the mother can absorb, or feel the fear and loss *for* the infant, those feelings, received and contained in the mother's mind, become less terrifying. As the frustration of the "no-breast/no-mother" becomes more tolerable, the infant's fear of the *absent* breast can be experienced as the *presence* of a "no-breast." This no-thing is essentially the *presence* of absence, creating a space in the mind where a thought – "no mother" – can exist. The mother's *emotional* presence ultimately makes it possible for the child to tolerate her *physical absence*, or separateness.

Bion (1963b) writes, "The thought owes its genesis to the absence of the object" (p. 18). Tolerance of the no-thing thus serves as the foundation of thought and the mind that can think it. The capacity to tolerate the reality of her absence reflects the infant's ability to tolerate the frustrations of loss and fear, an ability that develops only if the mother's mind can hold the infant's fear. This requires her to tolerate her own primitive fears of separateness, representing an evolved state in the mother.

In the mental space of "no-mother" or "no-thing," the mother's physical absence can be experienced as a *symbolic* mental presence of the absent mother, a symbolic "mother" able to be held in the mind as an image, later a word, representing her. If the mother is *emotionally* absent, unable to contain her own or the child's primitive fears, the infant's ability to create a mental space for the thought "no-mother" will likely be compromised and the development of thinking forestalled. Bypassing frustration for illusory satisfaction, the infant resorts to a hallucinated breast felt to be the thing-in-itself in a nonreal space, rather than a symbol in mental space.

Lacan similarly links the mother's act of naming things for her infant as leading to a differentiation of mother and child. He calls language "the murder of the thing," where the absent object stimulates the mind with a desire to substitute a word for the missing thing (Muller, p. 400–402). Lacan's idea reflects the emotional violence of feelings of separateness that are associated with the development of language.

The "No-Thing" in Early and Late Bion

As early as 1962, Bion describes a space in which resides a "no thing" [then unhyphenated] and links it to the capacity to think.

If there is "no thing," is "no thing" a thought and is it by virtue
of the fact that there is "no thing" that one recognizes that "it"
must be thought?

(Bion, 1962a, p. 35)

The answer seems to be yes, a thought is the absence of a thing *if*
the infant can tolerate the loss and terror associated with mother's
absence. Bion (1965) thus views absence as the essence of thinking,
that a thing cannot exist in the mind unless there is a corresponding
no-thing (p. 103). The no-thing can therefore lead either to the development of the mind or to its annihilation, antithetical outcomes determined by the infant's tolerance or evasion of frustration.

Either [the infant] may allow his intolerance of frustration to use
what may otherwise be a "no-thing" to become a thought . . . or
he may use what might be a "no-thing" to be the foundation for a
system of hallucinosis.

(Bion, 1970, p. 17)

Hallucination, he says, is "favoured for its immediacy" (ibid., p. 16),
instantly alleviating the terror of the mother's absence.

Clinical Example #1 – "Kate"

"Kate" was weaned at four months when her parents went on vaca-
tion. Left in the care of a nanny, Kate refused the bottle and cried
inconsolably for days, the beginning of a lifelong angry and distant
relationship with her mother. Both her parents, though, were also
detached from their feelings, which made it impossible to heal that
early loss.

Kate's anger and emotional deadness were apparent when she began
analysis. She was anxious, arrogant, and highly promiscuous, with
crippling symptoms of OCD. Because those previously recalcitrant
symptoms more or less disappeared in our first year of treatment,
Kate felt grateful to me and continued coming despite intense hostility toward me and the analysis. With those symptoms and her arro-
gance decreasing, feelings of emptiness emerged that often made her
silent and unresponsive. Any awareness of need for me or connection

lasted only for a few moments, or a couple sessions at most, before she again retreated to silent detachment. Currently, after twelve years of analysis, the fortress against feelings of need, despair, and abandonment of that original trauma surfaced in the transference. This led to intermittent feelings of love, which themselves felt traumatic to her.

In a recent phone session (during COVID-19), I answered the phone and said, "Hello." Imitating my inflection, Kate said, "Hello." I then said, "Hi," as one might in phone calls upon recognising the caller's voice. A long, eerie silence ensued. Finally, Kate said, "Your voice sounded friendly and warm." This was in no way positive, however; in fact, it disturbed her enormously, for my "warmth" was evidence that I was real, and thus outside her control, not, as she must have thought, her hallucinated breast/mother. Coming together with me at the beginnings of sessions had become very painful, in part because I, like her mother who disappeared in infancy, had disappeared physically because of the pandemic.

Recent Session

Although recently married, Kate's relationship with her husband was also intermittently unresponsive and distant. Lately, Kate sometimes remained largely silent for half the session, as she was in this Friday session. I finally said that she didn't seem interested in any contact with me today. She replied, "Nothing to talk about . . . I'm not aware of any problems." I said that we seemed to be at an impasse, and I mentioned her having raised the possibility in our last session of stopping analysis. I said, "If you really feel there are no problems, nothing I can help you with, and you want to stop, we can stop." She said, "I'll think about it."

On Monday, she was distraught at having reverted back to the sexual obsessions that had plagued her early in her analysis. She no longer acted them out and had lately described that on the rare occasions when they returned, they made her feel "crazy." For the most part, until today, they had completely disappeared.

> *My dream was disturbing. I was looking at computer porn, frantically searching for men . . . it was exciting. There was a woman*

there, I was kissing her but I was bored. She wanted to go to her place so I said ok, but I didn't really want to go. She looked fake . . . too much make-up.

"It was exciting. But then I woke up depressed at having these thoughts again." Kate is not a lesbian and did not know who the woman was. I asked about her "fake" look. "Like someone wearing too much foundation," she said, "the skin looks fake . . . too much foundation." She remembered the exciting sex with her first boyfriend, who eventually broke up with her without warning. "I cried for weeks," she said. When I reminded Kate that she often describes her mother as "fake," she replied, "Yes, and she wears too much make-up."

I thought that the possibility of stopping analysis had so terrified and saddened her that she attempted to make herself feel better, and avoid feelings of needing me, through sexually exciting phantasies. I also recalled having interpreted her fear last week of having no foundation for her personality. It disturbed her, and I said that I thought she now feels that in talking of such serious things, I have "too much foundation." I reiterated that while she doesn't have to talk to me, she also clearly *does* want to come, and this is the impasse she feels with me. She can't decide if she wants the truth about her lack of foundation or wants to cover it all up again with sexual excitement.

Although Bion's (1962a) idea of the "selected fact" is not discussed in depth until the next chapter, I say briefly here that it is an organising element in the session, a pattern that, once detected, brings cohesion to seemingly disjointed aspects of the session. In this session, the selected fact puts us in the realm of Kate's early loss and the defences she used to deaden her feelings. The idea of stopping analysis had reignited that trauma and Kate's terrifying awareness of needing and/ or losing me. Through the lens of that early trauma, I seem to be the lesbian "kissing her," a reference to her abrupt weaning, where the "oral sex" with her nursing mother had ended. Our "oral sex," or verbal intercourse in analysis, was similarly threatened by our discussion about stopping analysis. Like her association to her first boyfriend, who, like her weaning mother, ended the relationship "without warning," she fears that I am offering the same fake connection that will end up devastating her like her first failed attempt at connection with her mother. Like Winnicott's (1974) "fear of breakdown," Kate waits in dread for that early loss to repeat itself with me, and in fact she recreates it by her need to obstruct contact with me.

This is the foundation upon which Kate's life has been based, and so she continues to kill off her desire in our "oral sex" (talking with me). Her manic sexual excitement now makes her feel "crazy," but she is not yet familiar with sanity and so doesn't want to go to "my place" in the dream, in part because she fears the despair of another fake connection but also because she fears that "my place" is sanity and does not yet know what will happen there. She doesn't know if she wants emotional truth or the old lies that protected her from needing her absent mother. Reality versus hallucination is a difficult choice, for in this profound confusion, Kate cannot tell if I have too much foundation because I am fake or if I have too much foundation because I present her with painful truth.

At this point, the space for a no-thing keeps opening up but collapses in terrified reminiscences of a no-mother, the link to whom essentially died in Kate's mind at just four months, leaving her without a mental foundation to feel or think. This dream helped move us in that direction, and when she left, Kate said, with great vulnerability, "So we'll continue talking about it tomorrow?" "Yes," I agreed.

Kate stayed in analysis, and since then, instead of saying goodbye at the end of each session, she often says, "Till next time." This expression of need for and anxiety about losing me is evidence of a space between us and a space in her mind – the "no-thing – in which she can hold my absence "till next time." It gave me insight into the idea that Kate, deeply angry and arrogant for so long, was probably a particularly loving baby whose trust/love died at what felt like a terrifying betrayal. Any gratitude or need for me was extremely dangerous, but she now also keenly feels the dangers of the sexual defences that buried her real self and left her empty. We might say that in lieu of the capacity to think about the "no-thing," one is left with nothing.

No-Thing vs. No-Emotion

We've seen how inability to tolerate frustration can result from too much or too early loss and too little help in containing those feelings. Hallucination allays the infant's terror and helplessness but compromises or destroys the perceptions of internal and external realities. Bion (1970) writes, "A word representing a thought is not the same as the identical word when it is representing an hallucination" (p. 17). The word "mother" differs significantly for someone able to symbolise the absent object in thought and for someone for whom "mother" represents hallucinatory possession of the object. If the patient's words do not exist in the mind as symbolic thoughts, they have no meaning, and the space where the mind or self might be is collapsed, and "the emotion of the 'no-thing' . . . is replaced by a 'no-emotion'" (ibid., p. 19–20). The no-thing then gives rise, not to a mind or thought, but to mindlessness, as substituting hallucination for the absent no-thing leads to annihilation of time and reality.

> The "place" where time was (or a feeling, was, or a "no-thing" of any kind was) is then similarly annihilated. There is thus created a domain of the non-existent. . . . Some patients . . . achieve a state, to which I wish to apply the term "non-existence," for a few moments at most; this is followed by an . . . evacuation of "non-existence."
>
> (ibid., p. 20)

This helps in understanding Kate's silent states of nothingness, as searing, un-felt pain cauterises real human feelings. As her mind became like hardened scar tissue, feelings were sexualised, and Kate could feel only through her vagina until a mental space was created for emotional connection.

Bion (1970) makes a distinction between patients who can suffer pain and those who "feel the pain but will not suffer it and so cannot be said to discover it" (p. 9). The capacity to tolerate the frustration of the no-thing is fundamentally about the ability to suffer the reality of the mother's absence, without which one *has* loss but cannot suffer it. One cannot feel or remember the loss, but the loss "remembers" the patient through constant, confusing repetitions, like the sexual obsessions. Bion adds that if one can suffer pain one can also "suffer" pleasure, so the real issue is not pleasure or pain but the capacity for a mind able to tolerate the *reality* of feeling. If one cannot tolerate reality, pleasure is an equally unbearable reminder of the reality of separateness in the mother's absence.

Clinical Example #2 – "Ella"

"Ella" is a bright, sensitive woman who began losing weight as an infant when her mother's milk proved insufficient. Weaned at three months, she suffers from eating disorders and body dysmorphia, often feeling lost. The unconscious "conclusion" she seemed to reach from her early starvation was that her mother did not want her to eat and that food and hunger were bad. These precocious attempts at logic, before there is a capacity to think, endured, and her job as she sees it is to starve, the foundation of her anorexia. This keeps the depriving mother alive in her mind but also idealises the deprivation in an attempt to mitigate the enormous pain of needing something that was unavailable. While Ella's parents are loving people, there is a surprising absence of emotional awareness, which gave Ella no help in dealing with this complicated loss.

Despite all this, Ella has a sense of joy and fun, which I saw as evidence of having retained some primal connection to a healthy infant self, although deeply split from her feelings. She functions well but is driven by the unconscious yearning for a depriving breast, reliving that early loss in a kind of self-imposed emotional exile.

Ella's dreams were infrequent, disjointed, and confusing. I work every day with dreams, but these evoked in me few thoughts and little meaning, like unconnected images and unsorted, unfelt feelings. Never having "digested" the loss, confusion, love, and hate for this depriving mother/breast left no mental space to contain that first thought – "no-breast." Not surprisingly, her prohibition against needing also made it difficult for Ella to receive anything from me. When I interpreted her difficulty hearing me, she demurred, "But I feel like you're the only one who speaks my language." Because I speak about her feelings, Ella's hidden real self recognises that I speak her language, but I would say that Ella herself does not yet speak her own language. There is no open channel to reach that undamaged infant's real potential for a mind. While I felt an intuitive unconscious-to-unconscious communication with her, there was no mind available to process what I said.

As her deprivation became more conscious, Ella felt pulled into her infantile despair. I was faced with an impenetrable system of illogic with no real capacity to dream, or think, just her old convictions that she needed to starve herself. At one point, most sessions were filled with intractable self-hatred, berating herself for failing to fast. I pointed out that since we all need food to stay alive, her "failure" to starve herself actually represented her desire to live. This angered her, making her feel I didn't understand the necessity to starve.

Things progressed, however, and after four years of analysis, I was surprised to see a change in Ella's dreams. Their randomness and impenetrability gave way to patterns in which I detected feelings and meaning. I had never experienced such a dramatic change in a person's mode of dreaming, which seemed to reflect the existence of a space in her mind for feelings.

After another several months, her need to starve herself was challenged by some pleasure in eating, sitting down to proper meals, and dreams about food, ice cream, cooking, and family dinners. The no-breast had at times become a mental reality, able to be symbolised in dreams. As her ancient defences started breaking down, her fear led to a renewed determination not to eat. At times Ella no longer felt we were speaking the same language, for her language was again that of a punishing superego demanding that she starve to protect her from the pain of needing an unavailable, and now bad, breast. This deep confusion between good and bad was essentially a disorder in thinking, an entire belief system based on a false belief in avoidance of pain. The no-breast that cannot be digested had become the "no-emotion," annihilating Ella's emotional reality. The superego superself misuses the natural potential for logic and punishes her "*for her own good*," to kill the intolerable starvation of needing an absent breast. From this perspective, everything I said now felt dangerous. I had revealed her right to eat, to exist, while *her* aim was to stay emotionally dead.

Two Sessions

In this first session, Ella felt lost, while arrogantly asserting her conviction that what she really needs to feel her best is not to eat. I said that she believes she has all the answers and yet still feels lost and that while claiming to value our work, she is working hard not to need anything I say. Like her weaning mother, what I give her is not enough, and it is potentially painful. This interpretation disturbed her. "I don't understand what you're saying," she said. Her confusion about my interpretation felt to me like a subtle but positive change, for she was experiencing me for the first time as separate from her, a breast/mother whose food was "incomprehensible." However, she did not simply spit out my interpretation, she took it in long enough to think about it, and her thought was that it was incomprehensible. Not understanding implied a space for curiosity and potential understanding. While her *inability* to understand was not new, her *awareness* of it was.

In the following session, Ella said, "I thought about what you said. I think you meant that I keep putting in quick answers. . . . I really have to give up my old answers and try to listen to you." I said that apparently, she had done just that, listened and thought about what I said. While still perplexed, she heard me.

> *I dreamt I was waiting for my mom to come over with my aunt and her baby, so we could go for dinner. I wanted to shower. Since they were all at the beach, I thought, they'll have to clean up too before we go. But they arrived ready to go and had to wait for me, I was the one that wasn't ready.*
>
> *At the restaurant we sat at a table, the waiters brought food, but we were supposed to go to a different restaurant for dinner after . . . maybe we were here for a drink or snack. My aunt knew my mother had miscommunicated and said to her, "We can't just go there for cheese."*

Ella did not know why the waiters brought food so quickly. I suddenly thought that the key to this dream, the "selected fact," is the idea of *waiting*. First Ella is *waiting* for her mother and aunt; later they are *waiting* for her. Then the *waiters* do *not wait* but bring food Ella and her family cannot eat. Of course, the infant Ella was unable to wait for her mother's insufficient or absent food, and her way of not waiting was to stop needing food. I think her surprise in the dream that she was making her mother wait because Ella "was not ready" reflects her prior revelation about needing to take in what I say. She had always believed she had all the answers and could take care of herself, but there is an awareness here that in fact she was not ready, she needed help, and her unconscious "decision" as an infant not to need her mother was a lie.

In a sense, Ella's confusion about my interpretation in the previous session made her aware that we were speaking a different language. It made her aware of having to wait for understanding and to wait for our current session. Waiting is the central achievement of the "no-thing," for tolerating frustration in the mother's absence is essentially the capacity to wait. Ella's first comment in this session about giving herself quick answers made me think that the "waiters" who too eagerly bring food also represent that impatient, terrified infant whose capacity to wait was replaced by the fast food of fast answers, even if they are the wrong answers that destroy her pain and her mind. In this very condensed dream, the fast food is also a pun for her desperate need not to eat, to "fast." Like the impatient waiters who bring the food too quickly, this starved infant fed herself all sorts of lies but here has an inkling that just eating the "cheesy," insufficient, or soured milk is not enough.

After a lifetime of feeding herself bad mental food, Ella had enough faith to dare to taste something new – her profound lack of understanding about my interpretation and about her own mind. This dream was a very big step on a long journey, for it reflects an inchoate capacity to think. A space had been created between us, in which I was now a no-thing she might be able to wait for and think about.

Chapter 3

The Selected Fact

Bion's innovative theories about mental development led to a need for innovative clinical techniques. Given his theory that the infant's potential for a mind requires certain emotional conditions in relation to the mother in order to develop, if those conditions are not met, the psychoanalyst will need to find a way to communicate with that undeveloped, proto-mental mind. This revealed the need for specific, cogent interpretations able to reach those hidden or unborn selves. Bion's (1962a) "selected fact" is one of his most innovative clinical ideas, and yet, despite being central to his view of psychoanalytic practice, it is not often discussed. It seems very much related to Bion's (1965, 1970) other central clinical innovation – his concept of O, the essential psychoanalytic perspective – and the suspension of memory, desire, and understanding that facilitates access to O. While this is more frequently discussed, it is often amidst great controversy. Bion's early ideas are often seen to be so different from those of his late period that there is little to no connection between them, but I also examine here what I see as the continuity between the earlier "selected fact" and his later ideas, including O.

The selected fact addresses the analyst's challenge about how to make sense of the often-overwhelming plethora of stimuli in a session, in patients' words, feelings, associations, body language, dreams, etc. The question of how to find the "right" or cogent interpretation within that flood of stimuli is an aspect of Bion's (1977b) question about "how to get the interpretation to the right address." One cannot separate the content of one's interpretation from the person with whom one is trying to communicate.

DOI: 10.4324/9781003158509-4

Bion borrowed the term "selected fact" from French mathematician Henri Poincaré (1914), here reflecting on the creation of new mathematical formulae:

> [A new result] must unite elements long since known, but till then scattered and seemingly foreign to each other, and suddenly introduce order where the appearance of disorder reigned. Then it enables us to see at a glance each of these elements in the place it occupies in the whole.
>
> (quoted by Bion, 1962a, p. 72)

Much as the mathematician gleans relevant facts from a plethora of scientific data, the analyst must winnow the relevant idea that gives coherence to the seemingly foreign elements in a session. This idea implies the existence of a hidden but fundamental harmony that, if discovered, brings order to apparent disorder and forms the basis of a cohesive interpretation. According to Poincaré, without this harmonising element, the complexity of the world would overwhelm the mind.

> The only facts worthy of our attention are those which introduce order into this complexity and so make it accessible to us.
>
> (ibid.)

The challenge of finding order in chaos is familiar to any psychoanalyst working toward finding the central relevance in the verbal, emotional, physical, and metaphysical diversity of a session. Like the adage "You can't see the forest for the trees," the organising principle is right in front of us but obscured by all the separate parts. One must attend to those disparate parts without getting bogged down by the minutiae, allowing patients' communications to wash over one's mind without imposing premature meaning. Finding the selected fact is, to use another metaphor, like finding a needle in a haystack, a difficult mental discipline that requires what Freud (1909) called "evenly suspended attention" (pp. 111–112), what Keats (1817) called "Negative Capability" (pp. 328–329), and the waking dream state Bion (1967a, 1970) called the suspension of memory, desire, and understanding that facilitates contact with O. All these demand a more essential overview achieved by relinquishing control of logical thinking.

While Bion's (1962a) first mention of the "selected fact" preceded his concept of O, the ability to find that elusive analytic "needle in a haystack" of the selected fact depends on that deeply intuitive, and highly controversial, state of mind of O. The ability to detect the pattern in the selected fact is also similar to what Freud (1893) so admired in Charcot, his early mentor in diseases of the nervous system. Charcot would "look again and again at the things he didn't understand to deepen his impression of them . . . till suddenly an idea of them dawned on him" (p. 12). Bion's selected fact is a similar process of a sudden inspiration that helps detect the pattern embedded in the patient's material. This provides a sort of key to unlock the essential meaning of the session.

Looking back on his 1950 paper, "The Imaginary Twin," Bion (1967b) made reference to this sudden inspiration that he later called the selected fact, calling it "the coming together, by a sudden precipitating intuition, of a mass of apparently unrelated incoherent phenomena which are thereby given coherence and meaning not previously possessed" (p. 127). This "sudden precipitating intuition" also describes O. What sounds random actually requires faith and the patience to discover for oneself what may already be a known theory. It is not discovered, though, by "forc[ing] a theory to fit a realization" (ibid.). Rather, it is by tolerating uncertainty and surrendering one's mind to what was described by a 14th-century Christian mystic as "a cloud of unknowing" (Anonymous, 2020).

> When you . . . abide in this darkness [with] nothing in your mind but only God, and you look truly you shall find your mind not occupied in this darkness but in a clear beholding of some thing beneath God."
>
> (ibid., p. 31)

In Chapter 6, we get to the idea of how "God" figures into a psychoanalytic understanding of this state of mind, but the idea here is that in that dream-like cloud, the answer, or selected fact, may cut through the fog like a beacon. Like the cloud of unknowing, O is a waking dream state. Both involve suspending intellectual knowing in order to access more profound, intuitive awareness.

Seeing the selected fact as connecting Bion's early and late periods does not negate their differences or the revolutionary aspect of his later concept of O. Rather, it may provide insight into the already revolutionary nature of the earlier ideas that may have been overlooked. Looking with hindsight at Bion's work as one long session, I think O may be the "selected fact" that gave coherence to the otherwise diverse elements of his ideas about mental development. While O directly addresses the unknowable metaphysical mind, unmanifest in physical reality, it is access to this metaphysical mind that makes discovery of the selected fact possible.

Poincaré (1914) wrote, "What the true scientist alone can see is the link that unites several facts which have a deep but hidden analogy" (p. 27). This requires mental focus beyond sense-based, egoistic thinking and is consistent with Bion's description of O as the intuitive perspective of the genius or mystic. In 1962, Bion may not yet have had the theoretical understanding to describe the arcane, enigmatic state of mind of O, but his belief that it was possible to ferret out the essential truth of a session – the selected fact – indicates that he was able to think about that kind of laser-sharp, if inexplicable, intuition. O – absolute truth, ultimate reality, the infinite – might then be seen as a "thought without a thinker" that eventually found, in Bion's mind, someone to think it (see Chapter 4).

Bion insisted that he was not a mystic, but in also defining access to O as the domain of the "genius" or "exceptional person" (p. 74), he gave the idea a laical, non-religious perspective. O, it seems, was a silent partner in Bion's personality that fuelled the fertile imagination and prolific creativity his colleagues and students early on recognised as genius.

Clinical Implications

Like O, it is difficult, if not impossible, to describe how one intuits the organising function of the selected fact in the seemingly random ephemera of a session. And so how does one hope to express the means to do so? Britton and Steiner's (1994) paper "Interpretation: Selected Fact or Overvalued Idea" raises the question of how one can determine whether what one sees as the selected fact is in fact the relevant factor that unlocks the meaning of the session or simply a kind of delusional certainty born of a need to find an answer. The answer is at least addressed by Bion's idea of O, the need for contact with a more deeply intuitive mental state. Without this capacity to leave one's ego out of it by suspending memory, desire, and understanding, the analyst may simply be grasping at straws to allay the anxiety inherent in dealing with the plethora of stimuli in a session. Without O, in other words, apprehension of the relevant hidden organising factor is not possible. This is why Bion quotes Keats's "Negative Capability," a state of mind that precisely expresses the need to tolerate doubt and uncertainty by excluding the "irritable reaching for fact or reason." This, however, like O, represents a difficult mental discipline or talent for this temporary eschewal of logic.

I can give my own experience of ways in which the selected fact may make itself known to me. I sometimes experience it as a sense of something out of the ordinary, something striking or striking by its absence, a discrepancy that gives one pause or focuses one's attention by piercing that dream-like "cloud of unknowing." This is interesting in terms of Poincaré's statement that the aim is "not so much to ascertain resemblances and differences, as to discover similarities hidden under apparent discrepancies" (p. 21). I find at other times that it may feel like a special message, something particularly meaningful. It may come to awareness as a word or phrase or an ardent feeling, an idea in the patient's communications, a mental image, or anything that awakens a different kind of consciousness. Once alerted to it, it still may take a while to catch its meaning, or the coherence it brings to disorderly ramblings. I sometimes think of the session as an unwoven tapestry, whose unconnected individual threads are everything that occurs in the session. With the help of the selected fact, those loose threads, as if on their own, begin to unite to form a picture.

While it may sound mysterious, we all have the experience of subtle foreshadowing while reading a novel or watching a detective movie, a clue that suddenly shifts our perspective to provide a new perspective on "whodunit" or who is about to do it.

Before developing his concept of O, Bion's harmonising element of the selected fact pointed us in that direction, as did the discipline of suspending memory and desire that facilitates contact with O. These earlier outlines of what he later described as a mystical state make the presumed abyss between Bion's early and late periods seem less abysmal. O turns out to be the hub of a psychoanalytic revolution for which the foundation had already been laid, not by conscious design but as a function of that inherent underlying design Poincaré observed as a natural harmony, waiting to be discovered.

Clinical Examples – Selected Fact

"Richard" is a bright, intuitive professor and devoted husband and father. With a bi-polar mother and emotionally absent father, he spent much of his childhood alone. When he began analysis ten years ago, he seemed unaware of the emotional toll of this early neglect. He recently dreamt:

> *I came upon a man who had been killed. He was covered in a bloody sheet and I was terrified to look at him because I somehow knew the man had lost one quarter of his face. I was horrified, and confused, because I thought I had killed him, even though I just happened upon the body.*

Richard mentioned a book in which a murderer had "blown off a man's ear and a quarter of his face." His association to "masks" was to having seen Japanese theater, whose actors wore masks, which hid their feelings. He remembered hearing, as a boy, his mother's gruesome account of her childhood accident in which her face was badly abraded. He often didn't believe her tales and most of the time didn't even believe she was really psychotic, as if she were just pretending. As he got more in touch with his feelings, we could see that it was simply too painful to believe that he essentially had no mother to care for him. Richard also mentioned a recent "horribly uncomfortable" interview for a job, where he felt compelled to answer irrelevant personal questions.

The gory nature of this dream might make one think it was about Richard's violent, destructive feelings. In short, one might think all sorts of theoretical things that interfere with hearing what is essential to the particular moment. One could try to make a case for his murderous rage at his psychotic mother or at me for asking him uncomfortable personal questions that unmask him, interpretations that on another day might actually be to the point. But today, I felt nothing particularly hostile, just empathy and curiosity about Richard's confusion and guilt at thinking he had killed a man he had just happened upon. The question is, who is Richard today, and what is the selected fact that may lend coherence to help understand this session?

As I thought of the man in his dream, and in the book, who had lost "one quarter" of his face, together with Richard's associations to the mask, I suddenly thought that these victims of gory incidents had "lost face." This put us in the realm of shame rather than rage, and in this context, the dream seemed to reflect Richard's sadness and confusion about having lost his identity. Forced to conceal himself with a mask meant he had to hide, even from himself. If this is the selected fact, everything else should line up with this idea, and I saw that it was indeed the same story in his uncomfortable interview, having to reveal personal things to a stranger when he himself doesn't even know who he is. Earlier in the analysis, he often felt terrible discomfort when his feelings made him feel emotionally exposed to me, but again this did not seem to be the point today. This dream was about the confusion and shame of having inadvertently been forced to hide who he was, even from himself, making him feel that he was the one who had killed the man – his real self.

My idea of shame is that on a primal level, it is connected to an unconscious betrayal of one's authentic self (Reiner, 2022). Socrates, when asked if he was ashamed to have his life end the way it soon would, replied that he did not fear death, but dishonour, and to dishonour truth is to dishonour the self. The denial of one's guiding value was seen as the worst, or perhaps the only, source of shame (Plato, 1942). Unfortunately, this betrayal of one's essential self is not uncommon for children like Richard, whose true self is invisible to a mother unable to see them emotionally. The gory aspect of this dream aptly reflects the mental violence of "losing face," the deep shame of betraying, essentially killing, one's true self.

Once the selected fact – losing face – is revealed, it provides insight into the patient's mental state on that particular day. One then has a more cogent understanding of the patient's emotional story in that moment. It also provides needed evidence about whether or not one has read the dream, and the patient, correctly. Bion (1970) wrote, "The patient should be shown the evidence on which the interpretation is based" (p. 14). Whether or not one tells the patient everything, we at least have to provide ourselves with evidence that we are on the right track. In this case, the fact that it was "one quarter of the face" suggested to me that despite having endured enormous neglect and suffering, Richard had retained some fraction of his real identity, enough to have allowed him to retrieve as much of it as he has in analysis. This was consistent with my experience of him as someone whose innate regard for truth had kept him from joining his mother in madness.

These sessions with "Megan" also illustrate the selected fact. She is a highly intuitive woman with a strong spirit who endured a series of early traumas, beginning with a premature birth due to her mother's health complications. She spent weeks in an incubator separated from her ill mother and later endured her mother's anger and depression and her father's abusive rages. Despite the lingering challenges of these serious traumas, Megan worked through some deep primitive confusion, terror, and rage and now has success and meaning in her life as a painter. She finally established a relationship with her mother, from whom she had been estranged since adolescence.

Session #1

Megan described feeling scattered. Throughout the session I struggled to stay focused, perhaps sensing that "scattered" self. She described a visit with her mother, feeling happy to see her recovering well from a recent injury. Her mother's house had been renovated to accommodate her physical therapy, thanks in part to Megan's help. Her mother exhibited her usual coldness, however, and at one point Megan gently touched her mother's back as they walked in the garden, and her mother recoiled with alarm, demanding, "Why'd you do that?" Megan remained calm and replied, "Because I'm your daughter, and I wanted to show you some affection."

That night Megan dreamt:

> *I was walking with a man in a garden behind a house, I noticed the shutters on the windows. I reached down to remove some dead leaves from a plant, and the man eyed me warily, as if I were judging him. "I love gardening," I reassured him. "I just like touching the plants."*

Megan described having had a vision of her father's raging face the night before, and it scared her. She wondered if the man in the dream was her father, an abusive man. She had some rambling associations, and I found myself again unfocused, sleepy, and confused about the dream. In the last ten minutes of the session, I asked about the house and the shutters on the windows. I wondered why she'd included this detail. "They were open," she said, and then she remarked that her childhood home had shutters. I immediately got an eerie feeling and suspected that this was the selected fact. While Megan had been open and caring toward her mother, trying to express affection, what she actually felt was the pain of a closed, or "shuttered," mother. Two things convinced me that this was the selected fact. First was the feeling I had that I had described to myself as an eerie "shudder," and second was the hidden paradox of "open shutters." At the time I didn't think of my own sleepy "shuttered" eyes but later saw it as part of the same point. Megan had reverted back to trying to take care of her mother, an infant's attempt to create for herself a loving, open mother and to deny her profound sadness and disappointment of having a mother who is shuttered. Even the idea of her mother's renovated house reflected this, for such neglected children do idealise, or "renovate," their mothers. My sleepiness reflected Megan's unconscious pain and the eerie chill of having a shuttered, unfeeling mother who could not even recognise a caring gesture, as well as Megan shutting down her real feelings in favour of that "nice," though deadly, phantasy of a loving mother. I interpreted that she was asleep to her reality and dreaming her old infant dream, hoping finally to succeed in "renovating" her mother in the hope of being loved. While it was a man in her dream, her associations were to left both her mother's and her father's rage.

My attention was drawn to the minor detail of the shutters, so as we see, the selected fact can be significant for its seeming insignificance. Similarly, it is often believed that the mystical dream state of O is meant to yield some extraordinary mystical idea. Bion, on the contrary, said:

> I found that I could experience a flash of the obvious, one is usually so busy looking for something out of the ordinary that one ignores the obvious as if it were of no importance.
>
> (Bion, 1974, p. 103)

Session #2

This session, one month later, followed a break of two weeks. Megan spoke at length about people struggling with COVID-19. "Even Nature is struggling," she said. Moments later she was distracted by an inch-worm that must have crawled in from her garden and was crawling on her shirt. "A little bit of Nature," she said, implying that she had somehow summoned it to her. Megan's ultra-sensitivity often includes psychic intuitions and uncanny experiences, but today I felt that she was rambling, distracted by this creature walking across her. I noticed myself getting anxious that we would run out of time before the session even began. Megan described another disturbing visit with her mother over the break. "She was anxious, difficult, she wouldn't listen to me." Feeling overwhelmed and somewhat detached, as I thought she was, I asked, "What are you feeling now?" "Lost," she replied.

This felt like the first real thing she had said today. She then told me these dreams, both of which had occurred just before our break.

> *I was on the street where my mother lives. You were there. You said to me, "You're not hearing me." I had my ear to the ground trying to hear you, but you said, "That's not where I am, you won't hear me that way."*
>
> *A few days later I dreamt about two paintings I'm working on and thought, "Why haven't I finished anything in my life? I don't want to just drift through my life without finishing anything."*

I began to realise that Megan's seemingly tangential meandering about the inchworm was not only relevant, it was in fact the key to the session, and it was about her embryonic, unborn self, drifting in a time-less realm. Megan could not be present with me in the session because in my absence I had become the mother who prematurely booted her out of the womb and she was like that vulnerable crawling inchworm. I understood that she was stuck in a connection to a womb-me whose absence was life threatening, I could then understand my anxiety about her drifting. My feeling that we would not have time to have a session reflected her feeling of not yet having started her life.

Her concern that she "can't finish anything" is relevant to this per-spective that she cannot finish something she feels has not yet begun, for she was still adrift in that timeless past. It may seem odd to see a random event like a crawling inchworm as central to the meaning in a session, but her reaction to it was just another of the patient's associ-ations, which are also seemingly random.

Megan's keeping her "ear to the ground" to hear me was also related to this drifting embryonic dream state, an effort to hear or communicate with me in my absence. In the dream I said that she isn't hearing me, as in fact she could not hear me during the break, but her ineffective method of trying to hear me seems related to Megan's heightened sensitivity and intuition. Ferenczi (1932) described an impulse in sensitive and emotionally abandoned infants to reach a hyper-intuitive psychic state he called the "astra" (p. 207). He called these infants "wise babies," who essentially flee to the "stars" in an effort to locate the absent mother intuitively (cf. Reiner, 2017). While they do seem to find deeply intuitive states similar to seers and mystics, the problem with this is that Megan disappears into a kind of "drifting," dissociative state. At that deep level, this dream "on her mother's street . . . in her childhood house" represents her mother's womb, to which she retreats, still emotionally unborn. Trying to find me with those infantile methods, she gets lost in that timeless imagination.

I was reminded of a piece of contemporary art I saw years ago – a large bronze digital clock, but instead of the time displayed, for instance, as 5:07 or 11:30, or any other time of day, the clock read 00:00. It was an apt image for this embryonic, eerie nowhere-ness in which the patient is outside of time.

Summary

In trying to describe the way these mysterious selections of the meaningful harmonising element are made, Poincaré (1914) wrote, "Scientists believe that there is a hierarchy of facts, and that a judicious selection can be made" (p. 16). Just as scientists talk about the beauty of a theory or equation based on its simplicity, Poincaré also wrote,

> It is the search for this sense of special beauty, the sense of the harmony of the world, that makes us select the facts best suited to contribute to this harmony. . . . Thus we see that care for the beautiful leads us to the same selection as care for the useful.
>
> (pp. 22–23)

Poincare's statement is very much what Keats (1819) said in his famous lines from "Ode on a Grecian Urn":

Beauty is truth, truth beauty – that is all
    Ye know on earth, and all ye need to know.

We are looking for the harmony in the session because ultimately it reflects the harmony in the minds of the patients who dream these dreams. To hear the selected fact requires the intuitive waking dream state of the unknowable O, which starts with our having the faith and courage to face our own ignorance, to stop thinking about what we *know* so we can focus on learning what we *don't* know.

Chapter 4

Thoughts Without a Thinker

O and Thoughts Without a Thinker

Bion's (1977d) ideas about thinking later came to include what he called "thoughts without a thinker," wild thoughts that come to us unbidden, like dreams, while we are asleep or awake, but of which we cannot claim ownership or are not yet able to think. These intuitive, imaginative, ephemeral thoughts are the numinous thoughts of seers or mystics or strokes of genius in the minds of artists, scientists, or psychoanalysts. This is very much related to O, absolute truths that exert pressure on the mind to think them simply because they are true. Like "the elephant in the room," one can either notice or turn away from truth, but it is still the truth.

The selected fact is one example of a thought without a thinker, a hidden but fundamental harmony which can be detected by a mind open to the deeply intuitive state that Bion described as O. Once able to think it, the thought brings order to apparent disorder. Grotstein (2007) also describes the early theory of α-elements as the foundation of "'thoughts without a thinker' that have been thought all along by 'godhead' ('godhood')" (p. 62). The godhead, of course, was also represented by Bion as "O," and so despite the belief in a deep schism between the early and late periods of Bion's work, there are many chronological overlaps and theoretical elements linking O to many of Bion's earlier ideas. When Bion finally talked directly about O, the necessary state of mind in which to practice analysis, it was a quantum leap in what was thought to define psychoanalytic work but was nonetheless beholden to the states of mind he had earlier outlined.

DOI: 10.4324/9781003158509-5

The "no-thing" that creates a space able to contain the thought – "no-mother" – is the foundation of individuation, the basis of selfhood and mindfulness. Again, this idea predates Bion's articulation of O but relates to O as it reflects on the origins of the self, mind, and thinking, all of which are necessary *if that at-one-ment with O is to be useful in making psychoanalytic interpretations*. The unbounded state of at-one-ment with O is a function of the infant's boundaryless mind, making it possible without that more evolved thinking self. However, the infant, not yet capable of thinking, obviously cannot do the work of psychoanalysis, and so, as we see further in Chapter 6, the capacity to *use* the experience of O psychoanalytically requires a mind that can also transform the primal experience (O) into communicable thought.

Thoughts without thinkers are essential truths that exist whether or not anyone thinks them, and this too is part of the ineffable, absolute truth of O. O represents the infinite, unthought, and unthinkable thoughts of cosmic reality beyond our capacity fully to understand them. The universe guards its secrets from our finite minds but sometimes shares bits of its reality with geniuses like Einstein, who can think, or dream, these universal "thoughts." Einstein's thought experiments about time and space were the dreams and musings of a curious mind that gave the rest of us a tiny window into an infinite reality. Bion dared to dream that analysts too, in that dream-like state beyond memory and desire, could make contact with the unknown, O, with these ephemeral thoughts waiting to be thought. This "information" is part of the fabric of ultimate reality that cannot be fully grasped by our finite minds. Bion tries to describe our relationship to these unknowable facts: "Nobody needs to think the true thought. . . . The thinker is of no consequence to the truth, but the truth is logically necessary to the thinker" (Bion, 1970, p. 103).

Bion differentiates these truths, or organic thoughts, from false or non-thoughts, or lies, which exist only in the mind of the liar who creates them.

Whether the thoughts are entertained or not is of significance to the thinker but not to the truth. If entertained, they are conducive to mental health; if not, they initiate disturbance.

(ibid.)

Truth does not need us, but we most definitely need truth, which is the foundation of sanity. According to Bion (1970), thoughts precede our ability to think them, and our mental health depends upon our finding a way to do so. The "no-thing" is also an example of this, for the infant's emotional and physical need for the mother is an inexorable truth, a thought without a thinker that the infant must find a way to think. As we saw in the clinical examples prior, infants traumatised by the mother's absence and unable to tolerate the pain and loss create defensive "lies" of *not* needing her, omnipotent protections from intolerable realities, but the ensuing system of lies supplants the capacity to process truth, essentially destroying the development of a mind to think it.

Along these lines, Grotstein (2007) describes thoughts without a thinker as "inherent pre-conceptions" (p. 117), intuited ideas "known" before we have a mind to think them. These á priori truths are independent of experience. Truth itself, it seems, is an inherent preconception in the human mind, the "food for thought" that nourishes mental development. As we saw in the previous chapter, the infant's mental development depends on the ability to think that first "thought" – "no-mother" – the truth of which facilitates awareness of a separate self. Bion wrote: "*Thinking is a function forced upon the psyche by the pressure of thoughts, not the other way around*" (1967, p. 111, emphasis in original).

Heidegger (1971) similarly wrote, "We never come to thoughts, they come to us" (p. 6). New thoughts may come to the thinker whose mind is open to receiving these as yet untamed thoughts. Since the human mind needs truth to live, we need a way to think it, to be come open to what we do not know.

The Power of Truth

Bion preferred questions to answers, for answers were seen to close off curiosity and learning. Analysts were asked to relinquish the illusion of control, even over one's own ideas. The poet/philosopher T. E. Hulme (1929) wrote, "Prose is a museum in which all the old weapons of poetry are kept" (p. 15). Poems, like dreams, reflect an always newly invented form of language, created in the moment, often in order to express otherwise ineffable states. Like

Bion's distinction between the Language of Achievement and the Language of Substitution, Hulme describes two distinct languages, one powerful, the other somehow inert or past its usefulness. The "weapons of poetry" are potent, but once possessed or overly familiar, they become tired relics stripped of their potency. Familiarity and understanding can be deadly as we grow too comfortable with our theories. As Bion wrote: "Melanie Klein could not reconcile herself to the fact that whenever she had made herself understood, that fact rendered what she understood no longer alive" (1975, pp. 88–89).

Like the dusty relics in Hulme's "museum," we can study theories, turning them over in our minds admiringly, but they are no longer relevant. We cannot think with the relics of established facts when thinking is a dynamic function of mental energy that cannot be possessed or hoarded. Ideas must be discovered, then released, to make room for new ideas. Like the selected fact, truth must be discovered on the spot to find thoughts with the potency of those "weapons of poetry." The selected fact is the discovery of a new theory in each session, a thought without a thinker waiting for us to think it, and release it, to make room for the next thought.

Dreams as Unconscious Thinking

Grotstein (2007) refers to nightmares as thoughts that cannot find a thinker, a kind of mental indigestion of primal feelings that cannot be transformed into thoughts. I would call them thoughts *in search of* a thinker, for the nightmare actually *did* find a thinker, who happens to be asleep, whether in the dreamer and/or in the analyst's half-waking, half-sleeping mind.

Pirandello's (1921) play *Six Characters in Search of an Author* depicts a playwright's relationship to characters who have a life of their own beyond his control. Thoughts without a thinker are like those itinerant characters searching for an author to give them voice, purpose, and meaning. The analyst is at times like that author who simply translates the patient's unthought thoughts, or undreamt dreams, into thoughts.

My proposal that Bion's earlier ideas provide the foundation for the mystical O even before O was articulated is an example of a thought that had not yet found a thinker to think it. It eventually found a thinker in Bion, who conceived of the thought – O – that seems to have searched for him for years. O is a thought about the absolute truth that became central to his view of psychoanalytic work. But these unknowable intuitions needed the foundation of mental functions outlined in Bion's early theories in order to be known, communicated, and practicable in psychoanalytic practice.

Outside of psychoanalysis, the concept represented by O certainly was *not* a thought without a thinker, for this numinous experience beyond logical understanding had been well documented by artists, mystics, and scientific visionaries throughout history. Bion's O reflects these numinous experiences through the lens of psychoanalytic understanding, outlining ways to contact and interpret metaphysical mental states as aids in psychoanalytic practice. Psychoanalysis is an exploration of the unconscious, and so psychoanalysis *is by definition* the exploration of O. Our challenge is to catch up with Bion and find a way to think the previously unthought thought he finally managed to think, about applying these profound, numinous experiences to psychoanalytic work.

Art and Thoughts Without a Thinker

Apropos of Bion's (1962a) early idea that thinking develops "as a method or apparatus for dealing with 'thoughts'" (p. 83), many writers say that they don't write to *express* what they think, but rather to *find out* what they think, as their unthought thoughts are revealed to them. By relinquishing control to what artists call the "Muse" or "God," and Bion called O, the mind in that state of unknowing is receptive to thoughts it cannot yet think. It may feel as if the work is writing (or painting) itself, guided by some external or divine force, like Plato's view of poets as "nothing but interpreters of the gods" (Plato, 1961, p. 220). And Bion described what Keats called "Negative Capability", because it is the same kind of surrender to unknown essential truth.

Bion's ideas about lies are also among his most useful ideas in understanding mental functioning. We may see patients who function at a high level but whose primary mode of mental functioning is a lie. These unconscious lies are a mode of "thinking" that is not thinking, using "words" that are not really words, for they are not being used to communicate but to obstruct communication. Bion wrote: "The patient, especially if intelligent and sophisticated, offers every inducement to bring the analyst to interpretations that leave the defence intact and, ultimately, to acceptance of the lie as a working principle of superior efficacy" (1970, p. 99). This kind of resistance underlies Bion's (1978a) frequent observations about a seemingly fundamental hatred of thinking, a view of the mind itself as "a frightful nuisance" (p. 53).

Clinical Vignette

"Stella's" mother was a workaholic businesswoman, emotionally distant and narcissistic, and her stepfather was bi-polar. From early infancy, she was often cared for by housekeepers, and she struggled all her life with states of withdrawal and dissociation and a marriage characterised by distance. She has finally begun to trust me, which brings her intermittent hope and dread.

Stella felt connected to me in our last session, and so was hopeful, but she began today's session with a deadly silence, some endless blather, and then more silence. I felt, as I often do, a gaping absence, and I had sensations of being choked. She finally spoke about having been vaccinated for COVID-19 and feeling somewhat guilty since some older people could not yet get vaccinated. She mentioned, without concern, her disinterest in intercourse with her husband and spoke of flirting with a man at her yoga class, which used to excite her but no longer does.

> *I dreamt about my friend, Andy, a work friend, who said he refused to get vaccinated. I immediately lost respect for him and knew I could no longer be his friend.*

"I can't understand all these people, this is a deadly virus! I also lose respect for people who voted for Trump," she said, then clarified that in real life Andy would neither refuse the vaccine nor vote for Trump. I felt confused about Stella's dream and cannot say I disagreed with her belief that people need to get vaccinated. My mind drifted back to her deadly silence at the beginning of the session and her detached rambling, and I suddenly thought that the deadly virus against which Stella has been vaccinated was not COVID but "sex," not just genital inter-course but emotional intercourse, psychoanalytic intercourse, any kind of connection. From this perspective, she was long ago "inoculated" against connection, love, and life, all things she cannot understand. This, I thought, was the selected fact, for it seemed to make sense of a nonsensical situation. As mentioned previously, the selected fact is one version of a thought without a thinker, that can only be apprehended through deeply intuitive states, and with this idea of the selected fact, I interpreted that Andy represents me – her "work friend" – whom she feels is foolish enough not to have gotten vaccinated against life, sex, or connection, since I keep talking to her about these things. As a result, she wants nothing more to do with me. It explained the deadly silence and meaningless prattle at the beginning of the session, com-munications that were largely anti-communication, anti-contact, and I thought that her guilt at having gotten that anti-life vaccine in real life reflected her slowly growing interest in connection with me and the growing awareness of how damaging this emotional "vaccine" has been to her life and our work.

If I had been thinking logically, I would have missed the point. Given my own beliefs, I would probably have agreed with Stella that *not* getting vaccinated was foolhardy, but this would have missed the analytic point of her deeply held belief in being "vaccinated" against contact. The apparent logic of the dream essentially had to be turned upside down in order to hear the selected fact, the thought without a thinker, that Stella herself was turned upside down about whether contact with me (or anyone) was a good idea or a disaster.

Stella's inoculation against contact is understandable given her early maternal abandonment, but internally it now represents the unconscious edict of a deadly, primitive superego, attempting to pro-tect her from the pain of contact with an unavailable mother. At this point, she is in conflict about which she prefers, but knowing that Stella is emotionally "vaccinated" in this way gave us both more understanding of the power of her interdiction against contact and the serious obstacle it poses in our work.

Chapter 5

The Royal Road to O

Asked about O, Bion (1977c) said, "I find it useful to suppose that there is something I don't know but would like to talk about, so I represent it by O" (p. 33). Early on he said of O:

> What the absolute facts [of the session] are cannot ever be known, and these I denote by the sign O.
>
> (Bion, 1965, p. 17)

These last two chapters are dedicated to various aspects of O – the vast, ephemeral unknown of the human mind – and its association with the mystic, an association that made this concept a lightning rod for controversy.

The apprehension of O reflects matters of psychoanalytic theory and technique that are central to Bion's clinical perspective.

> The success of psycho-analysis depends on the maintenance of a psycho-analytic point of view . . . the psycho-analytic vertex is O.
>
> (Bion, 1970, p. 27)

This is a bold statement since it places this logically unknowable, indescribable reality at the centre of psychoanalytic work. Bion's attempts to define O – ultimate reality, absolute truth, the godhead, the infinite, the thing-in-itself (ibid., p. 26) – hardly help to demystify the concept, since these definitions are themselves indescribable metaphysical realities. I therefore compare O to various creative arts and sciences to help reveal, metaphorically, something of this ineffable

DOI: 10.4324/9781003158509-6

experience. As Bion (1978b) wrote, "All these various disciplines – music, painting, psycho-analysis and so on . . . are indeed engaged in the same search for truth" (p. 43).

Bion's O and Freud's Unconscious

Grotstein (2007) described Bion's work as "the new 'mystic science of psychoanalysis'" (p. 24), where O represents a mental state uniquely different from Freud's or Klein's ideas of the mind. He describes O as "beyond words, beyond contemplation, beyond knowing . . . [T] his Beyondness is within us as our unconscious" (ibid., pp. 121–122). We are, in other words, both physical and spiritual beings, so while O cannot be known logically, it is embodied within unconscious, proto-mental aspects of the mind, into whose numinous reality one might get a glimpse. Still, despite its ineffable nature, Bion clearly elucidates the means of facilitating contact with O – namely, in the dream-like state of mind of suspending memory, desire, and understanding. Although its association to mysticism makes O the most controversial of Bion's ideas, it is clearly one of his most important, for in representing O as the necessary psychoanalytic perspective, it is the essential foundation of his theoretical and clinical work.

There are similarities between O and Freud's (1905) infinite, timeless realm of the Unconscious, but there are also essential differences. Freud's Id represents a repository for unknown, unwanted, repressed impulses within the Unconscious, while O, also timeless and infinite, represents a more expansive, transcendent unconscious mind that approximates to the inherent knowledge of Jung's unconscious archetypes, knowledge that predates one's life but is carried as part of one's unconscious history (McGuire and Hull, 1977). Bion (1978b) likened these Jungian theories to his idea of "a primordial . . . fundamental mind" (p. 4), a proto-mental system that exists before birth (Bion, 1961).

Unlike Freud's chaotic, unconscious energy striving to satisfy physical instinctual impulses, Jung's unconscious is "centrally powered by an intentional . . . energic force that strives for more than instinctual satisfaction" (Stevens Sullivan, 2010, p. 50). Like O, this spiritual self is driven by an inherent proto-mental self with an essential need for truth.

Grotstein (2007) found Bion's perspective more "hopeful" (p. 38), for the "seething cauldron of negativity and destructiveness" (p. 37) of Freud's Unconscious does not include the positive aspect of a mind motivated by its inherent need for truth. O represents an epistemological instinct, the potential for knowledge of one's *infinite* self, one's godliness, from which one may become alienated. For Freud (1900), dreaming – "the royal road to knowledge of the unconscious mind" – was in the service of the pleasure principle, whose aim was to reduce tension, while Bion saw dreaming as unconscious thinking, a necessary means of processing reality. Grotstein (2007) writes, "Thinking itself is, according to Bion, essentially unconscious" (p. 47), and it requires contact with the waking dream state of O.

Development of this aspect of the mind, one's "godhood" (ibid, p. 135), may be obstructed by the mother's inability to contain her infant emotionally. We saw this in earlier clinical examples and again in the clinical examples that follow. Traumatised infants develop a false self as the mind contracts into delusions and omnipotent defences, forfeiting the potential for the emotional connection and openness to curiosity and awe upon which development of the mind, self, and sense of reality depend. Freud wrote: "Our present ego-feeling is only a shrunken residue of much more inclusive – indeed all-embracing – feelings which corresponded to a more intimate bond between the ego and the world about it" (1930, p. 68).

Freud seems to be saying that this is the normal ego-feeling and alludes to the idea of a more expansive self. However, his view of the unconscious as that seething cauldron of unacceptable impulses excludes this "more inclusive . . . all-embracing," boundaryless experience of O that is also the primal experience of an infant or fetus.

In many ways, Bion's O has more in common with Georg Groddeck's notion of "the It" than with the "Id," a term Freud (1923) borrowed from Groddeck, a medical doctor interested in Freud's work. Freud had enormous respect for him, and despite Groddeck's claim that he was not a psychoanalyst because his views essentially differed from Freud's, Freud replied, "I must . . . insist that you are an analyst of the first order who has grasped the essence of the matter" (E. Freud, 1960, p. 316). The difference is that Freud's Id is dominated by shameful, unwanted impulses, while Groddeck's "It" represents a natural source of health, a unifying force. For Groddeck (1929), the true self is not the ego – *das Ich* ("I myself") – but the expansive, unknowable It – *das Es* (p. 72). For Groddeck (1961), the ego was a "symbol of impoverishment" (p. 239), and the It represented "the sum total of an individual human being, physical, mental, spiritual" (p. vi). Consistent with the transcendent primordial fundamental mind of O, the "It" represented "the coherence of the universe . . . which endured from everlasting to everlasting" (Groddeck, 1929, pp. 36–38).

Religious Aspect of O

With O, Bion introduced the importance of the religious state of mind, a controversial notion in part because of Freud's (1927) view of religion as an illusion, a neurosis. It becomes less controversial, however, if one understands Bion's (1970) distinction between the reified, *external* God of religious institutions and the metaphysical experience of O as an *internal* godliness that is a natural part of the human mind.

Bion does not compartmentalise science, religion, psychology, and philosophy; each is a part of the human experience. Many psychoanalytic ideas were expressed by religious figures; in fact, even Freud's understanding that dream symbols reveal hidden unconscious states is reflected in Christ's idea of the need to use parables to symbolise otherwise indescribable aspects of metaphysical experience. The reification of Christ as God in the Christian gospels differs from the Gnostic view of Christ as a teacher of metaphysical knowledge, aspects of a human mind open to an experience of the infinite. The word "gnosis" derives from the Greek "to know," and the Christ in the Gnostic gospels is a teacher of that divine esoteric knowledge (Pagels, 1989). The Christ of the Christian gospels requires faith in an omniscient externalised deity, while the gnostic view, like Bion's O, requires faith in the existence of truth that one must learn through disciplined mental work. In the former religious view, one outsources one's own mind, one's curiosity, to that externalised deity, which obstructs one's capacity to think, while O, with a mind open to a profound unknown, facilitates the capacity to think for oneself (Reiner, 2009, 2012). For Bion, insight into that dream-like metaphysical mind – O – is not only the domain of prophets or mystics but of psychoanalysts.

O and the Oceanic Feeling

The experience of infinite reality – O – is unknowable to our rational, ego-driven, finite minds, but it can be *sensed* by an infinite self through an experience of at-one-ment. This is characteristic of the infant's primal oneness, the "oceanic feeling," of an unbounded psyche (Freud, 1930, p. 64).

In understanding the distinction between Freud's Unconscious and Bion's O, it is worth noting that Freud's use of the term "oceanic feeling" was in response to author Romain Rolland's description of what for him was a "religious feeling." Although Rolland expressed admiration for Freud's ideas on religion, he regretted that Freud had not "properly appreciated the true source of religious feeling," a limitless, unbounded "sensation of eternity" that Rolland said he was never without (E. Freud, 1960, p. 388). Freud greatly admired Rolland and so was troubled by his friend's view of religious *feeling*, not as an illusion, but as something that coexisted with logic and reason. Freud admitted to having no such oceanic or religious feelings in himself, telling Rolland, "Mysticism is just as closed to me as music. . . . It is easier for you [writers] than for us [psychoanalysts] to read the human soul" (ibid., p. 389).

This is a telling admission on Freud's part, and through Rolland, Freud seemed at least to entertain the existence of a primal mind beyond his awareness. It is important to note, however, that Freud's view of organised religion as an illusion does accurately portray the child's primitive idealisation of the father (or more likely the mother) as the omniscient reified God of religious dogma. However, this view omits the more evolved religious feeling of Rolland's "sensation of eternity" and of O. The child's idealised view of his parents as gods is on a separate developmental line that cannot extend to the transcendent godhead (O), a mental capacity that each individual must develop internally. Symington (2004) distinguished between "a false god," in line with Freud's view of the primitive idealised parent/God, and a more evolved "true god" representing an internal relationship to transcendent states of mind, like O (pp. 115–116).

Religious dogma often tames, ritualises, and sterilises the wild insights of the mystic, while the religious *feeling* of O is born of the chaos of primitive, psychotic thought processes that must be contained in thought without destroying the energy of that primitive mind. This describes Bion's idea of the relationship between container and contained – ♀♂ – discussed in the next chapter, which forms the basis of a dynamic mind. Dogma, whether religious or psychoanalytic, is the product of concrete thinking impervious to vital thought. The reified, anthropomorphic "God" reflects what Segal (1981) called a "symbolic equation," concretising the experience it is meant to represent symbolically. Characterising O as the "godhead" distinguishes this experience of oneness that opens the mind to the unknown from the identification with an anthropomorphic God.

The Controversy of the Mystic

Bion's (1970) idea that the analyst must focus his attention on O, the "psychoanalytic point of view" (p. 27), garnered intense criticism, even among many admirers of Bion's earlier contributions. Grotstein (2007) wrote, "O'Shaughnessy (2005) suggests that Bion had become 'undisciplined' in his later years" (p. 19). Others thought his later ideas lacked academic rigor or were evidence of his mental decline. These controversies often were centred around ideas about the mystic, even questioning whether Bion really meant O to represent a mystical state, which was deemed antithetical to science. Bion was clear on both counts:

> I shall use the term "mystic" to describe these exceptional individuals. I include scientists, and Newton is the outstanding example of such a man: his mystical and religious preoccupations have been dismissed as an aberration when they should be considered as the matrix from which his mathematical formulations evolved.
>
> (ibid., p. 64)

The issue is not whether O was meant to represent a mystical state but rather what *Bion* meant by the word "mystical." The confusion presumes a connection between mystical ideas and *institutional* religion, overlooking Bion's secular view of mystical states as instrumental to accessing transcendent mental states beyond sense-based reality. The latter encompasses religious *feeling* while excluding the ossified thinking of organised religion that speaks *about* mysteries without being immersed in the mysterious unknown. Messianic ideas represent new thoughts that threaten those who cannot think them, strokes of genius that may threaten the institutional status quo. Bion's messianic idea is O and therefore a threat. To invalidate its importance is to miss the point that Bion made about Newton, that Bion's "crazy" mystical ideas about O may be the basis and fulfillment of his work, rather than an aberration.

Critics of Bion's later theories often segregate them from his early theories, but this may overlook the ways in which they are connected to each other. In 1962, Bion described the selected fact, the organising factor embedded in a discursive or chaotic session, but this very much relates to his later description of "thoughts without a thinker," discussed in 1970 and 1977. Both require access to the unbounded mind of the mystic – O – that makes it possible for the thinker to think it. Grotstein related the selected fact to the thought that has always been there but cannot yet be thought, and this "'Thinker' goes by the name 'godhead'" (ibid., p. 76). He adds that godhood, or O, is "the thinker of the thoughts without a thinker" (ibid). The selected fact, or any innovative idea, is a thought that finally finds a thinker through the exercise of that state of mind of the godhead, or O. We see more evidence of this, that these ideas of early and late Bion are not only related, they define each other, and each deepens the meaning of the other.

Any new idea may be met with curiosity, wonder, and hope but also, or perhaps more often, with confusion, fear, derision, and contempt. This is certainly true of Bion's concept of O. His concept of "catastrophic change" even predicts this fear and hatred of the unknown, for is there any greater stimulus for fear than an infinite unknown that is infinitely out of reach? And what greater stimulus for envy is there than those for whom this realm is even nominally more within reach? One can kill the new idea, and the envy, by killing the messenger – the "mystic, genius or exceptional individual" who perceived it (Bion, 1970, p. 64).

The danger of new ideas as a threat to existing beliefs is reflected in all religions and philosophies. Christ offered assurance that he had not come to destroy the ideas of the earlier prophets but to fulfil them (Matthew 5:17). But even *fulfillment* of an old idea, though not completely new, represents a development or deepening of something already known, making it unknown and potentially frightening.

O, as discussed, was an attempt to extend and fulfil Freud's already revolutionary idea of a timeless, infinite unconscious within. Despite Christ's reassurances about honouring the truths that came before, he also announced his intention "not to bring peace to the world, but a sword" (Matthew 10:34). This makes the role of the mystic/genius a paradoxical one, much like Shiva, the Hindu God of creation *and* destruction. And as Bion (1970) wrote, "The mystic is both creative and destructive" (p. 74).

Whether with Freud or Bion or Christ, people both fear and make gods of their leaders. Bion wrote, "I doubt [Freud] appreciated the force of the messianic hopes aroused" (p. 76). The deep hunger for truth and knowledge fights with people's profound fear of change, a fear that often leads to idealisation of the admired person and sterilising their ideas in what seems like religious reverence but may be more like the fate of idealised heroes who were "loaded with honours and sank without a trace" (Bion, 1970, p. 78). It is their ideas that sink and the idea of truth that must be constantly revised by our courage to challenge old beliefs with newly learned truths. Analysis clearly reveals that everyone grapples with change, and whether the new idea is devalued or neutralised by idealisation, the rigidity of institutional rules can "crush the life out of the very reason for their foundation" (Symington and Symington, 1996, p. 183).

Bion's awareness of primitive assumptions of group members toward their leaders led him to resist that role of leader. Audiences were sometimes frustrated that Bion did not give them established theoretical answers, as if from an omniscient God, but rather left space that might stimulate them to think about it for themselves. Psychoanalytic knowledge was not static data to be passed along but a process of growth in a mind that was constantly evolving. It would be pointless to memorise Bion's truth when the goal is to find a way to think one's own essential truth.

Psychoanalytic Bias Against Religion

Bion equated "mystic" with "genius" and "exceptional individual," thereby removing it from a strictly religious context (ibid., p. 64). This view of mysticism is in line with Einstein's (1954) statement, "Science without religion is lame, religion without science is blind" (p. 55).

Psychoanalysts have been peculiarly blind to this topic of religion . . . [A]ctivities which can be called religious are at least as
obtrusive as activities which can be called sexual. . . . One won-
ders on what grounds a mind or personality could be regarded as
a human personality or character if it had missing one of the main
departments of mental activity.

(Bion, 1974, p. 15)

Freud's (1927) atheism, and his view of religion as "a mass delusion"
(p. 85), probably helped shape the antagonism between psychoanalysis and religion. He was interested in the occult, however, but chose
to put it aside, fearing it would tarnish the scientific reputation of
psychoanalysis. He even warned Ferenczi that publishing his paper
about such esoteric things would be like "throwing a bomb into the
psychoanalytical house" (Jones, 1957, p. 393), not so far from some
of the reactions garnered by Bion's mystical concept of O.

The fundamental concerns of religion and psychology are nonetheless similar. On the surface, the book of Genesis is an origin story
of mankind – God creates Adam, fashioning Eve from his rib, thus
straining the credulity of even the least scientific thinker. But from
a symbolic, psychological perspective, it represents the genesis of
consciousness, morality, and the human mind. Adam and Eve are
tempted to partake of the Knowledge of Good and Evil, the assess-
ment of which forms the basis of moral, and mental, development.
It is forbidden by God, but as we see here, seeking this capacity for
a more highly evolved mind also seems to be forbidden, even by
otherwise evolved human beings. This simultaneous need for and
resistance to truth and knowledge is an essential conflict that we
see often in our patients and ourselves. O calls attention to religious states often viewed as *supernatural*, or supra-human, attitudes
described by Bion (1970) as "a lack of experience of the 'natural'
to which it relates" (p. 48). What we see in the Bible as punish-
ments of a supernatural God are metaphors for *natural* functions
of a metaphysical human mind struggling for, and resisting, deeper
understanding.

The secrets of the mind do not give themselves up easily, but Bion
clearly kept trying to find a way toward more understanding. Bion
wrote: "The term 'science,' as it has been commonly used hitherto

to describe an attitude to objects of sense, is not adequate to represent an approach to which 'psycho-analytical science' has to deal" (1970, p. 88).

Royal Road to O – Suspending Memory, Desire, and Understanding

Psychoanalytically, Bion suggests, the royal road to O is through the analyst's suspension of memory, desire, and understanding. Since memory focuses on a past that is already gone and desire on a future that does not yet exist, one is left only with the present. This temporary suppression of ego functions stimulates a boundaryless, dream-like state that breaks down ego boundaries to facilitate the sense of "at-one-ment" with the patient's experience. This poem by Pessoa is a fair description of the suspension of memory and desire and O:

> What matters is . . . to know how to see without thinking,
> To know how to see when seeing
> And not think when seeing
> Nor see when thinking.
>
> But this . . .
> This requires deep study.
> Lessons in unlearning . . .

(Pessoa, 1914, p. 57)

Suspending memory, desire, and understanding is a way of temporarily unlearning what one knows, thus creating the mental space for something new. Again, this is the realm of the artist, and Picasso also asserts the artist's on-going need to break with tradition and conventional standards of beauty in the search for truth. (Gilot, 1990).

Although relinquishing control is part of the experience of suspending memory, desire, and understanding, it can be frightening. This fear of letting go is evident in the painter's fear of the blank canvas or the writer's fear of the blank page, coming face to face with the unknown. Bion (1965) describes it as the dread that accompanies contact with reality in psychoanalysis.

Resistance is resistance to O. Resistance operates because it is feared that reality is imminent.

(p. 127)

Because O is inherently mysterious, it is often believed that the state of suppressing memory and desire always yields very extraordinary or impressive new ideas. And yet Bion wrote:

I found that I could experience a flash of the obvious, one is usually so busy looking for something out of the ordinary that one ignores the obvious as if it were of no importance.

(Bion, 1974, p. 103)

That is what one is waiting for – the obvious, the simple truth that had somehow eluded awareness – but if one can stop trying, it may emerge to be seen.

Dreaming: Awake or Asleep

Bion (1978a) called O "a peculiar state of mind . . . [where] the margin between being consciously awake . . . and being asleep, is extremely small" (p. 41). The analyst may doze off, sometimes "drugged" by powerful unconscious projections of a patient's unfelt feelings. This is not simply falling asleep in the session. Suspending memory and desire is not a dead sleep but a rigorous mental discipline that can lead to profound intuition.

It is easy to . . . slip over into sleep . . . It is equally easy to slip over into a state of being horribly intellectually awake. The border between the two, the correct state of mind, is very difficult to achieve; one is always oscillating above and below it. Being on the right wavelength . . . is unfortunately comparatively rare.

(ibid.)

Bion compares this state of mind to states of ego regression that feel like the death of the self. He suggests that this is not an endeavour for beginning analysts, who must first have their own primitive paranoid schizoid and depressive anxieties analysed before attempting to enter this state of mind, akin to the sensory deprivation in dreams. The difficulty of this discipline led Bion (1970) to quip: "A bad memory is not enough: what is ordinarily called forgetting is as bad as remembering" (p. 41).

Bion examines the meaning of wakefulness – usually associated with reason, sanity, reality – and dream states that seem unreal or even insane.

> We have a prejudice in favor of the W [Waking]-state. . . . Who decides the priority of the W [Waking]-state over the S [Sleep]-state?
>
> (Bion, 1979, p. 327)

This suggests that some waking states actually reflect a mind that is asleep and some sleep states are necessary to being awake.

Clinical Example – "Rosa"

"Rosa" is intelligent, engaging, and functions well in a creative job. She was always an overachiever in school, and while she seems highly logical, it became clear that her "thoughts" were often obsessive ruminations that led nowhere. A traumatic premature Caesarean birth left her too early separated from her mother for several weeks, and she later was prematurely weaned as well. Although her parents were loving people whom she loved, they seemed to have no sense of emotional life and seemed blind to the feelings of their sensitive daughter. Despite her sensitivity and intuition, I often had the sense of someone with no inner world.

At first Rosa rarely dreamt, and when she did, she rarely had associations. I felt her emotional distance and deep sense of meaninglessness, and while I managed to make a few tentative interpretations, I felt uncertain that I could reach her. Something apparently got in, and several years into her treatment, her increasing vulnerability had led to more anxiety at times, but I also felt the presence of a real person.

In this first session after a Christmas break, Rosa spoke of feeling lonely over the holiday, saying she wanted a romantic partner and needed a new work partner. When she mentioned "our last session before we broke," I realised that she felt, in my absence, that our partnership had broken.

> *I dreamt I was at my parents' house . . . my parents and brother*
> *were asleep. I was outside, I felt heaviness in my chest, a dark*
> *presence. I tried to call out, "Daddy, help me!" but I had no*
> *voice, I couldn't move. It was so real . . . I didn't know if it was a*
> *dream or was really happening. I saw a tiny dot in the distance,*
> *a light maybe . . . I didn't know what it was. Was I supposed to go*
> *toward it? But I couldn't move.*

As she spoke about the dream, I thought it probably *was* real, a proto-mental, unremembered "memory" that had been repeating her whole life. Her nightmare of being alone started with her birth when she found herself, as in this dream, "outside" her mother's house, outside the womb. Being weaned so early again left her painfully left outside of her mother, who could not contain her infant's dread. As in the dream, her mother was essentially asleep to the darkness, heaviness, and loneliness of Rosa's terror. The "partner" she was so desperately looking for was a mother who could receive her terror and confusion. I remarked that she seemed to have deep feelings as an infant but no idea what they were. After a long pause, she said, "I felt I had to save my family, but I didn't know from what." In order to have a partner, she would indeed have needed to save her mother.

Without a partner to contain and give meaning to her mind, Rosa had fallen emotionally asleep, leaving her, as in the dream, paralysed, with no voice, no awareness of a self. I interpreted that, in my absence, she felt I too was a sleeping partner, but I thought that on the eve of our coming together again, the tiny light was a distant memory of our connection before we "broke" and my ability to be a partner for her feelings. As in the dream, however, she did not know what this light was or who I was.

She said, "But I know you understand." I did think that knowing she was returning today for our session was that glimmer of light that her terrified infant self could not recognise. It left her in the dark, petrified and bereft, with no way of knowing who or what she was. Bion expresses this dilemma:

> Reality is not necessarily pleasing or welcome. . . . We can be in
> a universe of thought, a culture . . . of such a kind that we are sure

> to suffer the pain of feeling that universe is not conducive to our welfare . . . we may be disposed to get out of [that universe]. . . . If we cannot . . . we can be reduced to other forms of escape – like going to sleep, or becoming unconscious of [this] universe.
>
> (Bion, 1979, p. 322)

While Rosa's achievements in life were impressive, on that proto-mental level, she had escaped the "universe" of her family by unconsciously putting her real feelings to sleep. As she became aware of being lost, that old nightmare awakened and became real, but the enigmatic light in this dream was one sign of beginning to see into that dark infantile confusion.

Clinical Vignette – "Rachel"

"Rachel" endured unspeakable neglect and abuse as an infant and young child. In the first ten minutes of this session, I had trouble concentrating on what Rachel was saying. This is unusual for me, and I knew something was being expressed that I did not understand. She told me this dream:

> *I was driving my car and realised I couldn't control the brakes. I was completely terrified that I would crash. But suddenly the brakes were okay and it was alright. I was so relieved.*

She said a lot more, talking about her new car, the first really good car she ever bought for herself but which she almost never drove because of the pandemic. She mentioned a terrifying incident while biking down a hill, thinking the brakes had gone out, and she spoke of her mother's disregard for her feelings, a torment for Rachel since infancy. None of this seemed to align with the relief at the end of her dream. It was still hard for me to concentrate, and after a long time, I suddenly sensed that instead of her "brakes," this dream had to do with Rachel's "breaks." Once I thought this, everything fell into place, and I could see that the positive outcome in the dream was actually negative. As an infant, careening into feelings of terror and helplessness with no brakes, feeling out of control, Rachel's terror simply *breaks* her mind. So when she says that "suddenly the 'breaks' were okay," it means that once her mind breaks and is splintered, everything is okay, for she can no longer *feel* the terror or helplessness. There is no longer a mind or self able to feel anything, including the fear that she is now fragmented. My confused, detached, sleepy feeling as she spoke today reflected this, for I had absorbed the unconscious fragmentation, the utter absence of a mind or anything able to contain what she felt – nothing made sense.

Here, the selected fact is the idea that the "breaks" were okay, but by dreaming of this otherwise hidden reality of her breakdown that had been neutralised and turned good, we could begin to see the obstacle to her getting better. What felt to me like mindlessness, and falling into sleepy stupor, felt to her "okay," a relief. By embracing the "breaks," she continues to rely on that dissociated state to find relief from the feelings she has never been able to feel.

Summary and Conclusions

New ideas that bring change can be shocking and frightening, and the idea of needing access to an unknowable O is, for some, one such shocking psychoanalytic idea. It is shocking in part because in order to become one with the noumenon, the thing-in-itself, the analyst must eschew reason. This is a fundamental change in analysis, for as Bion (1974) said, "What Freud and psychoanalysts have investigated is phenomena" (p. 41).

The egolessness of O is uncomfortable for both analyst and analysand, as it is for artists who deal with the terror of the blank canvas or blank page that can stifle creativity. De Kooning (1949) compared the blank canvas to the void in Genesis, out of which God creates the world, and he described his experience of giving over to this egoless state as being "utterly lost in space forever" (pp. 15–16). According to Bion, it is nonetheless a necessary capacity for psychoanalysts as well, imperative in the apprehension of the selected fact that helps uncover meaning in a session. This is the revolution in Bion's idea of O, for according to Bion (1975), failures to achieve this central psychoanalytic perspective are "breaches in the analytic frame of mind" (p. 37–38). This is not knowledge that can be learned through logic and intellect but rather a discipline through which one gradually develops a tolerance for not knowing, for keeping an open mind, by trusting one's own capacity for truth. I think we can describe O as Bion's messianic idea, which even now, forty years after his death, continues to challenge psychoanalysis to a deeper level of feeling and thinking.

Chapter 6

Continuity in Early and Late Bion

An Integrative Approach

O and the Mystic

Bion's (1970) idea of mysticism reflects emotional states of reverence, awe, and transcendence that are not traditionally religious or supernatural. Rather, they are seen as natural, though perhaps unfamiliar, aspects of mental functioning that are mistaken as supernatural. Symington (1998) defined primitive religion as one that "makes a god or gods the cause of those events which affect man" (p. 7). It is the devotion to an external God, either punishing or bountiful, that is felt to control the fate of humans. Freud's idea of God as the omnipotent parents, mentioned in the last chapter, would be an example of a primitive God. This differs from Symington's idea of a mature religion, which is internally directed by a capacity for the transcendent state of mind. Bion's O is an example of the latter, an evolution of the mind's natural religious feeling (ibid., pp. 14–15). While both primitive and mature religions reflect similar feelings of awe toward an unknown infinite world beyond our grasp, mature religious feeling is not felt to be a relationship to an anthropomorphic deity to whom people must pray or make sacrifices out of fear for their fate. O is that vast elusive order we can only marvel at but which far surpasses our capacity to understand it. It includes the unknowable order of our own minds, a mental universe that, as Freud showed, is largely unconscious. However, a mature religion like that of the Gnostic Christians who viewed Christ as a teacher of esoteric reality can be taken over by primitive beliefs that are institutionalised, like the Christian Church that reified Christ as a God with superhuman powers. While Bion claimed not to

DOI: 10.4324/9781003158509-7

be a mystic himself, he was most certainly a genius, especially if we apply his definition of genius:

> Genius has been said to be akin to madness. It would be more true to say that psychotic mechanisms require a genius to manipulate them in a manner adequate to promote growth or life.
>
> (Bion, 1970, p. 63)

For Bion, genius is the *use* of, not the *absence* of, psychotic parts of the personality, in the sense of primitive mental functions, taming the otherwise untamed energy of that primal, infinite mind in the service of growth. It requires a distinction between uncontained, unthinkable paranoid-schizoid anxieties and the capacity to transform those raw primitive experiences (what Bion called "beta elements") into the capacity for dreaming (through alpha function), by which thinking becomes possible. Contact with O represents contact with these disorganised primitive states in fluid relationship with more organised mental capacities. In the relationship between madness and genius, genius courts the "madness" of untamed emotional life and then harnesses this wild mental energy like a windmill provides energy by harnessing the wind. The primal unconscious is the source of mental energy that the genius, mystic, or creative person exploits to good use. For the analyst, contact with O facilitates access to the patient's uncontained mental energy and seeks to harness it in a vital thought – an interpretation.

Some analysts have suggested that Bion confuses O with psychosis. Blass (2011) describes O'Shaughnessy's criticism that O takes on "multiple contradictory meanings and ultimately becomes confused (e.g. mixing rapport with the godhead and psychosis)" (p. 1082). However, the confusion as to whether O represents psychosis or "rapport with the godhead" is not due to lack of discipline in Bion's thinking but to a lack of understanding of the paradoxical facets of an infinite mind to which Bion called attention. It reflects the discipline of a mind evolved enough to suspend ego functions of memory, desire, and reason and open the mind to an experience of natural states of hallucinosis, described by Bion (1970) as "always present but overlaid by other phenomena that screen it" (p. 36). He continues,

> By eschewing memories, desire, and the operations of memory,
> [the analyst] can approach the domain of hallucinosis.
>
> (ibid.)

The godhead, is not psychosis, for it requires the simultaneous strength of another part of the mind able to withstand the natural, primal states of hallucinosis in the mind without going mad.

O facilitates at-one-ment with the patient's experience, and some analysts view this as sufficient, without the need for verbal interpretations of that which has been intuited through this oneness with the patient. For Bion, however, O needs to evolve to the point where the analyst can interpret something specific in the process of helping patients contain their experiences in thought. Bion associates O with the mystic's intuitive vision, but in order for these intuited experiences to be psychoanalytically useful in creating and communicating interpretations, they must intersect with the containing capacities of the mind as described in Bion's earlier theories of thinking. It then becomes available as knowledge – what Bion represented by "K" – that can be communicated.

> It is O when it has evolved sufficiently to be met by K capacities
> in the psycho-analyst. . . . Insofar as the analyst becomes O he is
> able to know the events that are *evolutions* of O.
>
> (ibid. p. 27)

The Dynamic Mind – Ps ↔ D and ♀♂ (Container/Contained)

The foundation of thinking is not "intellect" as is popularly believed but in this ability to experience and dream the mind's primitive "madness," thus transforming them into thoughts. One is never "cured" of this primal "madness," which is part of the energy of mental life and thinking. Bion (1963a) proposed that these primitive paranoid-schizoid and depressive anxieties oscillate continuously throughout adult life and are part of the dynamic process of thinking, which includes the capacity to make analytic interpretations. Bion denoted these mental oscillations as "Ps ↔ D," indicating the transitions back and forth between uncertain disorganised states (Ps) and more integrated mental states (D) that are "part of the development of the capacity for thought" (p. 42). To be cured of this "madness" would mean being cured of having a mind.

Bion later described how these oscillations between Ps ↔ D were essential to analytic work and that both must be at work in the analyst's mind within every analytic session. He reframed the idea in emotional terms, calling the analyst's transition from disorganised states of unknowing to a more organised state a transition from "patience to security" (Bion, 1970, p. 124). One had to exercise *patience*, tolerating the discomfort and confusion of one's own paranoid-schizoid anxieties in order to reach a sense of *security* that came with deeper understanding in the session, as one transcended one's own ego through at-one-ment with the patient's experience. The analyst's clarity can be passed on to the analysand in the form of an interpretation.

> No analyst is entitled to believe that he has done the work required to give an interpretation unless he has passed through both phases.
>
> (ibid, p. 124)

The analyst does not control these on-going dynamic transitions in the mind. In the ways already described, one must first relinquish control to that cloud of unknowing, armed with faith that the truth, and the selected fact, will emerge. The selected fact cannot be consciously selected any more than one consciously selects the symbols in one's dreams. Instead, this is a state of patience, or faith. Again like Keats's (1819) "Negative Capability" ("being in uncertainties, mysteries, and doubts, without any irritable reaching after fact and reason"), it is equivalent to the dream-like state of O. For Bion, as described previously, it is not faith in an omnipotent God but faith in the existence of truth – the godhead.

Thinking itself, then, depends on the on-going relationship between contradictory states of mind – represented by Ps ↔ D. Another of Bion's (1963a) early theories, container/contained (♀♂), also represents the fluctuating, bi-modal mental functions that form the basis of a thinking mind, in this case the relationship between mental contents and the container that can hold them. This is an idea of a "mind" that is not a static entity that one *possesses or controls*; it is, rather, a process of mindfulness that is continuously created in the dynamic union of opposing, but cooperative, mental functions. Bion's daring question, mentioned previously, about whether psychoanalysts believe in the existence of the mind reflects this dynamic mind and a capacity to think that awaits further human evolution, a kind of thinking that is still "embryonic even in the adult and has yet to be developed fully by the race" (Bion, 1962a, p. 85).

The paradoxical nature of the mind is suggested in Bion's idea that an uncontained, disorganised paranoid-schizoid state can also function as if it were a form of container ($\female$).

> In sum, the two mechanisms [$\female\male$] can each operate in its characteristic manner or in a manner typical or reminiscent of the manner of operation of the other.
>
> (Bion, 1963a, p. 43)

Bion also talks about similarities between the functions of container/contained $\female\male$ and Ps $\leftrightarrow$ D and how each can assume the kinds of operations of the other.

> The operation Ps $\leftrightarrow$ D is responsible for revealing the relationship of thoughts already created by $\female\male$.
>
> (Bion, 1963a, p. 37)

The relationship between $\female\male$ is the foundation of thinking. While these overlays of mental functions are difficult to grasp, both functions reflect the cooperative relationships between different mental functions that are the basis of a dynamic mind. Bion also points out the paradoxical fact that seemingly incoherent dreams can also contain the selected fact that brings coherence to them. In other words, the coherent thought that the selected fact reveals in such a dream may be about the incoherence in the patient's mind.

I think we can understand this fluid relationship of seemingly opposing, bi-modal mental functions with reference to Fairbairn's (1952) structural model of the mind, based on his idea of the inseparable oneness of the mind's content and structure. The energy of the mind's contents, fuelled by emotions, is thus inseparable from the structure of the mind as a container for that emotional energy.

This is familiar to us in the arts as a union of form and content. In Jackson Pollack's "drip paintings," for instance, he created a completely new form to express the wild emotional energy that was also the content or subject of his paintings. Samuel Beckett (1953), in his play *Waiting For Godot*, created a completely new theatrical form, a meandering, seemingly absurd form that reflected the existential angst and confusion that was also its content. This integration of form and content is a mark of genius, expressed by Bion as the integration of psychotic thought processes with reason. We see it too as the capacity for fluid integration of opposing or bi-modal mental functions, a hallmark of the kind of mental integration expressed in Bion's early theories of ♀♂ (container/contained) and the fluctuations of Ps ↔ D. What begins as duality becomes a dynamic interplay of forces in the mind, a fluid dance between aspects of mental functioning that is the essence of a creative mind. This is the revolutionary aspect of Bion's early theories of thinking, a different sort of mind that is a necessary precursor to the later revolution of O.

Early and Late Bion

O seemed to have been evolving in Bion's mind for a long time before he found a way to address this expansive state of mind directly. Here we examine more closely what I think is their interdependence, presaged in those fluctuations of ♀♂ (container and contained) and Ps ↔ D. Both reflect Bion's version of a mind based on access to primal mental functions, and both depend on incorporating the infant's oceanic, dream-like oneness, central to the more evolved capacity to suspend memory and desire, that facilitates an experience of O. In this and other ways we will look into, Bion's later work seems to be both a revolution *and* an evolution, ideas that are different from, but essential to, each other.

While the relationship between O and the early theories is not causal, linear, or obvious, these early mental functions are necessary to the digestion of truth and the health of the mind. ♀♂ is a bi-modal function that must work together if the mind is to function in a healthy, creative way. Klein (1958) described the infant's need to reconcile paranoid-schizoid splits between a good and bad mother and good and bad aspects of the self. The classic duality between an emotional, chaotic Dionysian self and the rational logic of an Apollonian self is a part of us for which there are no ultimate resolutions, just on-going engagements with our own dual nature. Bion's (1962a) early idea of "binocular vision" is another example of a need to "correlate two views of the same object . . . conscious and unconscious" (p. 86). These simultaneous views of inner and outer realities help bring the mind into a unified perspective derived through cooperation between these dual functions. Grotstein (2007) similarly described alpha function as a combination of "primary and secondary processes . . . derive[d] from the cooperative bimodal binocularity" (p. 291).

Eshel (2019) calls O a revolution in psychoanalysis, a "paradigm change" (p. 8), and Grotstein goes even further.

> The concept of O transforms all existing psychoanalytic theories (e.g. the pleasure principle, the death instinct, and the paranoid-schizoid and depressive positions) into veritable psychoanalytic manic defenses against the unknown, unknowable, ineffable, inscrutable, ontological experience of Ultimate being.
> (Grotstein, 2007, p. 121)

Grotstein's assertion is a bold statement about the revolutionary nature of this much debated, much misunderstood concept. I agree wholeheartedly that O is revolutionary in psychoanalysis, and it may seem so different from the earlier work that its relationship to earlier ideas is not obvious. It may be especially difficult to see the ways these two periods are connected, however, if we overlook the already revolutionary ideas in Bion's earlier theories of thinking that essentially redefined what it means to have a mind.

Early and Late Bion – An Integrative Theory

The continuity of ideas that I am putting forth is based on the relationships between different states of mind that are dependent on each other. The new idea may transform how we understand the earlier ideas. So while it seems that the dream-like reverie of O is fundamentally different than the state of mind underlying Bion's earlier theories of thinking, according to Bion, the dream-like alpha function, at the foundation of thinking, is also an essential aspect of O. Thinking *is* dreaming, and the roots of O lie in the primal oceanic oneness of the infant mind, from which the mother's capacity for reverie develops, that can contain those early experiences. Bion (1977d) later describes "wild thoughts" or "thoughts without a thinker" that one may feel the need to "tame," by thinking them (p. 28). Like dream thoughts, they come to us while "asleep," or half asleep, for the capacity to tame or think them requires receptivity to the same waking dream state that facilitates access to O.

This would seem to make O a missing factor that Bion needed to develop in order to define what was necessary to the kind of vital mind described in the early theories of thinking. Bion is calling attention to what is needed to develop the potential for a human mind, to become human, and he makes it clear that mental health depends upon the ability to contain and process truth. Whether in the form of elusive thoughts without a thinker or O, it depends on the ability to transform primal emotional states of mind into thoughts through alpha function.

The Infant Is Not an Analyst

Although O, the necessary psychoanalytic perspective, reflects access to the unbounded, oceanic mind of the infant, infants do not make good psychoanalysts. Nor do psychotic people, so dominated by primitive psychotic mental processes that they cannot make use of them. Again, access to the infantile experience, and to psychotic thought processes, is a necessary but insufficient condition for doing analysis. The analyst must be capable of access to that unbounded infant mind, but the ability to make use of what is intuited through O requires the further development of a capacity to think, outlined in Bion's early ideas about the mother's reverie, alpha function, container and contained, etc. The analyst must be capable of the on-going transformations between ♀♂ and Ps ↔ D, between infant and adult. From this perspective, these very different mental states representing two periods of Bion's work are irrevocably dependent on each other. O represents an infinite reality that is a natural primal state of the infant's mind, but its relevance in psychoanalysis depends on its relationship to the capacities of thinking outlined in his early theories.

The ideas of what we might call an early "Apollonian Bion" were the more traditionally logical treatises that were acceptable to the logical science of psychoanalytic thought. The late "Dionysian Bion," on the other hand, has sometimes been seen as irrational, dreamy, mystical (in a derogatory sense), or "less scientific". This ignores the fact that he earlier described the containment of primal psychotic thought processes as the basis of logical thinking through the dreamlike alpha function and states of hallucinosis that continue as a sort of background to our minds. While embracing the mystical unknowable O is revolutionary in psychoanalysis, Bion's real revolution may be the challenge for analysts to be simultaneously identified with both sanity and madness, logic and chaos. He indicates this clearly in his definition of genius as the need to use psychotic mental processes in a way that promotes mental growth and health.

Bion's Legacy – O or K

Intuitive knowledge gained through the transcendent experience of at-one-ment with O is a completely different state of mind from K – knowledge gained through the senses (Bion, 1963a). However, the infinite mind (O) needs that sensory-based thinking about phenomenal reality (K) to make unthinkable noumenal states thinkable and communicable to the patient. From this perspective, K is a necessary but *in*sufficient factor in interpretive work, but O is also a necessary but *in*sufficient factor in analytic interpretation. As with ♀♂, what is relevant is the *relationship* between the two.

Grotstein describes O as a meeting between "infinite man" and a finite self that "longed to be realized in and by real human emotional experience" (2007, p. 37). We are not infinite minds *or* finite bodies, we are both, and mental life is the product of their working together.

A different perspective is expressed in a series of discussions about the controversy concerning Bion's early and later work. Blass (2011) quotes O'Shaughnessy's description of O as "less disciplined" and her view of "the instinct to know – the K link" as Bion's most important contribution (p. 1082). Mawson (2011) similarly described Bion's work of the 1940s to 1960s as "vigorously disciplined . . . [after which] . . . Bion's thinking becomes less disciplined . . . mixing and blurring categories of discourse, embracing contradictions, and sliding between ideas rather than linking them" (p 34). I think, however, that given the complexities of the mind described by Bion, a *different* mental discipline is required of the analyst – namely, the capacity to embrace precisely those contradictions.

Concerning the question of primary importance of O versus K, I think the answer is neither O nor K, but both. It is not a matter of choosing between transcendent intuition or sense-based knowledge but of cultivating a fluid relationship between these contradictory states of mind. Neither is more central or more important if what is central in psychoanalytic work is the relationship between them. Bion's challenge calls for the evolution of a mental bridge between the finite and transcendent self.

Regarding the criticism that Bion courted confusion by "sliding between ideas," what may be perceived as sloppy or undisciplined reflects a need to *tolerate* the inevitable sliding about between antithetical states without losing one's mental footing. Contradictory elements of the mind – finite/infinite, Ps $\leftrightarrow$ D, $\female\male$ – represent constant fluctuations between opposites underlying a dynamic mental life that is neither fixed nor predictable. The analyst's capacity for a relationship between antithetical mental functions is necessary for the clinical work Bion suggested, whether the suspension of ego functions of memory and desire or the intuitive receptivity to the selected fact. Logical thinking alone, or intuitive access to O alone, is not enough.

> Every object known or knowable by man . . . must be an evolution of O. It is O when it has evolved sufficiently to be met by K capacities in the psycho-analyst.
>
> (Bion, 1970, p. 27)

Psychoanalytic interpretations necessitate that transformation of O to K, where dream-like intuitions into numinous O evolve to a point where they reveal something to us of the known, phenomenal world. O is beyond words and might more effectively be represented by a dance or piece of music, which is not practical in most psychoanalyses. Still, while K capacities cannot fully formulate the absolute truth of O, only through this transformation O to K can the analyst represent O sufficiently to make a verbal interpretation that can be communicated and received by the patient.

Transformation of O to K

> The psycho-analyst is concerned with O, which is incommunicable save through K activity. O may appear to be attainable by K through phenomena, but in fact that is not so. K depends on the evolution of O →K.
>
> (ibid., p. 30)

Maintaining the perspective of O – beyond memory, desire, and understanding – is a formidable task in itself, but that alone does not allow the absolute truth of a shared moment of O to be formulated. It is in the evolution of O to K that the analyst can formulate something of that ultimately unknowable truth to himself and to the patient.

The idea of a relationship between O and Bion's earlier theories does not negate the revolutionary meaning of O, but I think it does cast the earlier theories into a new light, in the revolutionary view of what it means to have a mind that, like O, is an unknowable mystery. Without the foundation of a capacity to feel and think, described by Bion in $♀♂$ and Ps ↔ D, there is no mind or self available to contain the transcendent experience.

Some analysts find O to be meaningless or unnecessary, while others believe that this first step of at-one-ment with the patient is in itself sufficiently therapeutic. While this deep level of rapport or at-one-ment is critically important, it does not preclude the need to interpret what is intuited, allowing the patient to begin digesting previously unthinkable thoughts and feelings in the process of developing a mind.

The Mystic and the Psychoanalyst

Mystical thought and science, Bion points out, are not mutually exclusive. For the mystic to communicate with the common man, or with the common aspect in oneself, the unknowable O must be allowed to evolve to a point where it can be known.

> The religious mystics have probably approximated most closely to expression of experience of [O]. Its existence is as essential to science as to religion. Conversely, the scientific approach is as

essential to religion as it is to science and is as ineffectual until a transformation from K ⇒ O takes place.

(ibid., p. 30)

The point at which Bion's early and later theories can be seen to work together is in that transformation of K to O and then of O to K. Kant similarly wrote, "Thoughts without content are empty, intuitions without concepts are blind" (quoted by Bion, 1976, p. 316). At some point, the analyst's focus must shift from metaphysical at-one-ment to sense-based, evidential, scientific knowledge, from ephemeral noumenon to physically evident phenomenon. Without transforming the deep insights of that primitive O into knowledge through more ordered aspects of their minds (K), those intuitions may not be effectively communicated.

I have observed similar difficulties in patients with these kinds of exceptional intuitive gifts. They have no problem being one with O, but despite their often brilliant perceptions, they often cannot trust or make use of what they intuit without a mind able to process and give meaning to their primal intuitions (Reiner, 2004, 2006, 2017).

Clinical Example – "Danielle"

This highly intelligent woman had multiple early traumas, including early separation from her mother due to her mother's depression. Her father's emotional distance and abusive anger further contributed to "Danielle's" severe anxiety and terror of abandonment. However, these early traumas also gave rise to the kind of unusual sensitivity that Ferenczi (1932) associated with emotionally deprived infants, calling them "wise babies" (p. 81) because of their uncanny intuitive gifts. Such babies take flight from unthinkable pain into what he called "the astra" (ibid., pp. 81–82, p. 207). The astra is a state of mind like O, with access to transcendent wisdom, but since it reflects an attempt to escape the unbearable pain of an emotionally absent mother, this escape to the "stars" is also essentially a dissociative state. Danielle often described a sense of "scanning the universe," desperately searching for something, that we could later see as her earliest attempts to find her absent mother. In this escape to "the astra," the boundaryless oceanic mind experiences oneness with the universe, an openness to intuitive perceptions by which one gleans information. It is much like O, which provides the psychoanalyst with profound intuitions, but without a self or mind able to process the information. These uncanny mystic intuitions can nonetheless give them the mystical air of omniscient gods (cf. Reiner, 2017).

Danielle's "scanning" through the astral plane led her all over the world. In one session, she dreamt of a sad little boy, sweetly singing, "Where are the reindeer? Where have they gone?" I had no sense of what this meant, but I found that these prophetic, astral dreams often fail to stimulate associations as they are beyond the patient's personal experiences. Two days later, however, I read news reports, as did Danielle, that almost three hundred Norwegian reindeer had died that day. Huddled together in a storm, one was struck by lightning, and they were all killed. Danielle was often psychically drawn to catastrophic events like this, seemingly contacting them in the infant's "cloud of unknowing" where information exists beyond our usual experience of time and space, in a proto-mental, collective unconscious.

The prototype for these apocalyptic losses was Danielle's desperate need to find her absent mother after her birth. It is impossible to know just what these uncanny psychical feats are or how time and space can be breached at these mystical levels. However, knowing about the role of early trauma that destroyed contact with a patient's emotions enabled me to focus on the various feelings that gave rise to these mental forays into the astra. At one point I had said to her that her well-developed intuition took her far away but she hadn't yet found a way to live on the earth, to live in her body and mind. By now, Danielle has more contact with her feelings, and while she still has access to these transcendent states, she is no longer free floating in the astra.

The analyst in touch with O must transcend logic and ego boundaries in a similar way, but the necessary next step of a transformation of O to K necessitates access to an emotional self and mind described in Bion's theories of thinking. While society traditionally assumes the primacy and superiority of ego knowledge – K – our capacity to think is based on the primacy of the intuitive emotional reality – O – and the capacity to transform emotional life through dreaming. Bion here expresses the mysteries of O and its relationship to K:

O may appear to be attainable by K through phenomena, but in fact that is not so. K depends on the evolution of O $\Rightarrow$ K. At-one-ment with O would seem to be possible through the transforma-tion K $\Rightarrow$ O, but it is not so. The transformation O $\Rightarrow$ K depends on ridding K of memory and desire.

(Bion, 1970, p. 30)

Once divested of memory and desire, K becomes part of O, part of that waking dream state, with access to its numinous information. He also seems to be saying that without O, there is no K. This is in line with the idea that O is first and foremost the infant mind, from which all the rest evolves.

Summary and Conclusions

Although the concept of O was not yet manifest in Bion's earlier the-ories, his own transcendent mind presumably energised and directed him, perhaps inexorably, to that silent partner in his early work – O. He had already conceived of a new idea of a dynamic, sentient mind, of thinking that was the product of the dream-like alpha function, essentially dreaming one's feelings into a form able to be thought. The infant's mental development first of all depends on the dream-like reverie of the mother's mind, which allowed her to receive (to dream) her infant's emotional experience. While he could not predict where it would take him, he ended up at O, a transcendent version of that dream-like reverie.

The analyst's contact with O depends upon an adult mind still open to the dream-like oceanic feeling of the infant. The infant's oceanic feeling differs from the analyst's use of O, which depends on an estab-lished self, able to feel and think. That feeling/thinking self or mind is necessary in transforming O to K, which is perhaps the nodal point of continuity or connection between the ideas of Bion's early and late periods.

This means that if the mystical state of O is to be useful in psycho-analysis, one must first have developed a self or mind that can contain feelings, the basis of a thinking mind. Bion's (1970) advice that inex-perienced analysts refrain from that discipline of suspending memory, desire, and understanding until their own primitive mental states have been analysed indicates that one cannot safely or effectively enter that waking dream state of O without having developed a mind or self able to withstand the temporary impoverishment of the sense-based ego. Otherwise, one may simply be regressing to the infantile state, which seems like a sort of idealisation of empathy, a fusion with the patient's mind without the capacity for an observing ego. Having a self may seem like a low bar for an analyst, but in fact, in Bion's terms, it is a lofty goal reflecting the development of the capacity to think.

With O, Bion addresses directly the unknowable transcendent mind, as distinguished from the experience of institutional religions that speak *about* the transcendent God without direct experience of it. It is unlikely that Bion could have conceived of O as a useful psychoanalytic tool without first having conceived of the ways in which feeling states were transformed into thoughts through dreaming. O is that waking dream state, and as Bion points out, we are always dreaming. The analyst's mind has to be receptive to think the patient's thought or feeling through the proto-thoughts that come to a mind that is, like O, "nearly awake and nearly asleep" (Bion, 1977d, p. 29).

That infinite mind of O without a finite self to bring meaning to one's earthly or personal emotional existence is like a universe without gravity to hold the planets in orbit and keep us on Earth. Bion's exacting theories of thinking may have helped him develop a foundation in his mind – the gravity, and gravitas, that kept him grounded enough to make his daring journey into a new universe of psychoanalytic thought.

References

Anonymous (14th Century). (2020). *The Cloud of Unknowing*. Ed. C. Patel. Las Vegas, NV: Lamplight.

Beckett, S. (1953). Waiting for Godot. In *The Complete Dramatic Works* (pp. 7–88). London: Faber and Faber, 1986.

Bion, W. R. (1959). *Cogitations* (p. 43). London: Karnac, 1992.

Bion, W. R. (1961). *Experiences in Groups*. London: Tavistock.

Bion, W. R. (1962a). *Learning from Experience*. New York: Basic Books.

Bion, W. R. (1962b). A theory of thinking. In *Second Thoughts* (pp. 110–119). New York: Jason Aronson, 1967.

Bion, W. R. (1963a). *Elements of Psychoanalysis*. New York: Basic Books.

Bion, W. R. (1963b). The grid. In F. Bion (Ed.), *Taming Wild Thoughts* (pp. 4–22). London: Karnac Books, 1997.

Bion, W. R. (1965). Transformations. In *Seven Servants* (pp. 1–183). New York: Jason Aronson, 1977.

Bion, W. R. (1967). A theory of thinking. In *Second Thoughts: Selected Papers on Psycho-Analysis* (pp. 110–119). New York: Jason Aronson.

Bion, W. R. (1967a). Notes on memory and desire. *Psychoanalytic Forum* 11/3: 271–280.

Bion, W. R. (1967b). The imaginary twin. In *Second Thoughts* (pp. 3–22). New York: Jason Aronson.

Bion, W. R. (1970). *Attention and Interpretation*. London: Karnac.

Bion, W. R. (1974). *Brazilian Lectures I*. Rio: Imago Editora Ltda.

Bion, W. R. (1975). *Brazilian Lectures II*. Rio: Imago Editora Ltda.

Bion, W. R. (1976). Evidence. In F. Bion (Ed.), *W.R. Bion, Clinical Seminars and Other Works* (pp. 312–320). London: Karnac, 2000.

Bion, W. R. (1977a). *Private Meeting*. Bion's office, 435 N. Bedford Drive, Beverly Hills, CA.

Bion, W. R. (1977b). *Clinical Seminar. Bion's Home*. Los Angeles, CA: Homewood Road.

Bion, W. R. (1977c). 5 July 1977, Seminar 3. In *The Tavistock Seminars* (pp. 29–38). London: Karnac, 2005.

Bion, W. R. (1977d). Untitled, 28 May 1977. In F. Bion (Ed.), *Taming Wild Thoughts* (pp. 27–38). London: Karnac, 1997.

Bion, W. R. (1978a). 4 July 1978, Seminar 5. In *The Tavistock Seminars* (pp. 53–56). London: Karnac, 2005.

Bion, W. R. (1978b). *Four Discussions with W. R. Bion*. Strath Tay, Perthsire, Scotland: Clunie Press.

Bion, W. R. (1979). Making the best of a bad job. In *Clinical Seminars and Other Works* (pp. 321–331). London: Karnac, 2000.

Bion, W. R. (1991). *Memoir of the Future, Book II, The Past Presented*. London: Karnac.

Bion, W. R. (2005). *The Tavistock Seminars*. London: Karnac.

Blass, R. B. (2011). Introduction to 'on the value of "late Bion" to analytic theory and practice.' *International Journal of Psychoanalysis* 92: 1081–1088.

Britton, R., and Steiner, J. (1994). Interpretation: Selected fact or overvalued idea. *International Journal of Psychoanalysis* 75: 1069–1078.

Cookson, W. (Ed.). (1975). *Ezra Pound: Selected Prose*. New York: New Directions.

De Kooning, W. (1949). A desperate view. In T. Hess (Ed.) (1968), *Willem de Kooning* (pp. 15–16). New York: The Museum of Modern Art.

Descartes, R. (1637). *Discourse on Method*.

Einstein, A. (1954). *Ideas and Opinions*. New York: Random House.

Eshel, O. (2019). From extension to revolutionary change in clinical psychoanalysis: The radical influence of Bion and Winnicott. In *The Emergence of Analytic Oneness: Into the Heart of Psychoanalysis* (pp. 237–272). London: Routledge.

Fairbairn, W. R. D. (1952). *An Object Relations Theory of the Personality*. New York: Basic Books.

Ferenczi, S. (1932). *The Clinical Diary of Sándor Ferenczi*. Ed. J. Dupont, trans. M. Balint and N. Z. Jackson. Cambridge, MA and London: Harvard University Press, 1995.

Ferenczi, S. (1988). Confusion of tongues in adults and children: The language of tenderness and compassion. *Contemporary Analysis* 24: 196–206.

Freud, E. (Ed.). (1960). *The Letters of Sigmund Freud, 1873–1939*. New York: Basic Books.

Freud, S. (1893). Charcot. In *S.E.*, 3: 11–23.

Freud, S. (1900). The interpretation of dreams 2. In *S.E.*, 5: 608.

Freud, S. (1905). Three essays on the theory of sexuality. In *S.E.*, 7: 125–245.

Freud, S. (1909). *Analysis of a Phobia in a Five Year Old Boy*.

Freud, S. (1923). In the ego and the Id. In *S.E.*, 19: 3–66.

Freud, S. (1927). The future of an illusion. In *S.E.*, 21: 3–56.

Freud, S. (1930). Civilization and its discontents. In *S.E.*, 21: 59–145.

Gilot, F. (1990). *Matisse and Picasso: A Friendship in Art*. New York and London: Doubleday.

Groddeck, G. (1929). *The Unknown Self*. London: C. W. Daniel.

Groddeck, G. (1961). *The Book of the It*. New York: Knopf and Random House.

Grotstein, J. S. (2007). *A Beam of Intense Darkness: Wilfred Bion's Legacy to Psychoanalysis*. London: Karnac.

Heidegger, M. (1971). *Poetry, Language, Thought*. Trans. A. Hofstadter. New York: Harper & Row.

Hulme, T. E. (1929). *Notes on Language and Style*. Ed. H. Read. Washington, DC: University of Washington Chapbooks.

Jones, E. (1957). *The Life and Work of Sigmund Freud*, vol. 3. New York: Basic Books.

Keats, J. (1817). Letter to George and Tom Keats. In P. De Man (Ed.), *The Selected Poetry of Keats* (pp. 328–329). New York: New American Library, Signet Classic Poetry Series, 1966.

Keats, J. (1819). Ode on a Grecian Urn. In M. H. Abrams (Ed.), *The Norton Anthology of English Literature*, 4th ed., vol. 2 (pp. 825–827). New York: W.W. Norton & Co., 1979.

Klein, M. (1921). The development of a child. In *Contributions to Psycho-Analysis, 1921–1945* (pp. 13–67). London: Hogarth, 1950.

Klein, M. (1958). On the development of mental functioning. *International Journal of Psycho-Analysis* 39: 84–90.

Matthew 5:17, Gospel of Matthew. In *The Jerusalem Bible: Reader's Edition*. New York: Doubleday & Company, 1966.

Matthew 10:34, Gospel of Matthew. In *The Jerusalem Bible: Reader's Edition*. New York: Doubleday & Company, 1966.

Mawson, C. (2011). *Bion Today*. London: Routledge.

McGuire, W.; Hull, R.F.C. (Eds.) (1977). *C.G. Jung Speaking: Interviews and Encounters*. Princeton, New Jersey: Princeton University Press.

Meltzer, D. (1984). Dreaming as unconscious thinking. In *Dream Life: A Re-examination of the Psycho-analytical Theory and Technique* (pp. 51–70). Perthshire: Clunie Press.

Milton, J. (1652). Sonnet 19. In J. S. Smart (Ed.), *The Sonnets of Milton*. Glasgow: Maclehose, Jackson and Co., 1921.

Muller, John P.; Richardson, William J. (1982) *Lacan and Language: A Reader's Guide to Écrits*, International Universities Press: NY.

Pagels, E. (1989). *The Gnostic Gospels*. New York: Vintage Books.

Pessoa, F. (1914). *In Fernando Pessoa & Co.: Selected Poems*. Ed. R. Zenith. New York: Grove Press, 1998.

Plato (345 B.C.E.). (1942). Crito. In B. Jowett (Trans.), *Five Great Dialogues* (pp. 65–84). Roslyn, NY: Walter J. Black.

Plato. (1961). Ion. In E. Hamilton and H. Cairns (Eds.), *The Collected Dialogues of Plato* (pp. 215–228), Bollingen Series LXXI. Princeton, NJ: Princeton University Press.

Poincaré, H. (1914). *Science and Method*. London, Edinburgh, Dublin, and New York: Thomas Nelson and Sons. In (2012). *Forgotten Books*, www.forgottenbooks.org.

Reiner, A. (2004). Psychic phenomena and early emotional states. *Journal of Analytical Psychology* 49: 313–336.

Reiner, A. (2006). Synchronicity and the capacity to think. *Journal of Analytical Psychology* 51: 555–575.

Reiner, A. (2009). *The Quest for Conscience and the Birth of the Mind*. London: Karnac.

Reiner, A. (2012). *Bion and Being: Passion and the Creative Mind*. London: Karnac.

Reiner, A. (2017). Ferenczi's 'astra' and Bion's 'O': A clinical perspective. In A. Reiner (Ed.), *Of Things Invisible to Mortal Sight: Celebrating the Work of James S. Grotstein* (pp. 131–148). London: Karnac.

Reiner, A. (2022). Shame and the betrayal of the self. In J. Langham (Ed.), *Contemporary Klein and Bion in Los Angeles: Developments in Psychoanalysis*, vol. 2. London: Phoenix Publishing House.

Segal, H. (1981). Notes on symbol formation. In *The Work of Hannah Segal: A Kleinian Approach to Clinicval Practice* (pp. 49–68), New York: Jason Aronson.

Stevens Sullivan, B. (2010). *The Mystery of Analytical Work: Weavings from Jung and Bion*. London: Routledge.

Symington, J., and Symington, N. (1996). *The Clinical Thinking of Wilfred Bion*. London and New York: Routledge.

Symington, N. (1998). *Emotion and Spirit: Questioning the Claims of Psychoanalysis and Religion*. London: Karnac.

Symington, N. (2004). *The Blind Man Sees: Freud's Awakening and Other Essays*. London: Karnac.

Winnicott, D. W. (1960). Ego distortion in terms of true and false self. In *The Maturational Processes and the Facilitating Environment Maturational Processes and the Facilitating Environment* (pp. 140–152). London: Karnac, 1965.

Winnicott, D. W. (1974). Fear of breakdown. *International Review of Psycho-Analysis* 1: 103–107.

Index

Made in United States
Troutdale, OR
12/03/2023